THE CURRENCIES OF THE HINDU STATES OF RAJPUTANA

THE CURRENCIES OF THE HINDU STATES OF RAJPUTANA

BY

WILLIAM WILFRID WEBB M.B.

SURGEON CAPTAIN INDIAN MEDICAL SERVICE
BENGAL ARMY

Illustrated by a Map and by Twelve Plates of Coins after drawings made by the author from specimens in his collection

GYAN

Published by

GYAN

Gyan Publishing House
5, Ansari Road
Daryaganj, New Delhi-110002
Phone: 011-47034999, 9811692060
E-mail: books@gyanbooks.com

Distribution Network
gyanbooks.com
India, USA, Canada, UK, Australia, France

ISBN : 978-81-212-2712-4 (HB)
First Published, 1893

2nd Impression 2021

Printed at: Gyan Press, Delhi.

The
Currencies of the Hindu States of Rajputana
Author: William Wilfrid Webb

THE
CURRENCIES OF THE HINDU
STATES OF RÁJPUTÁNA

BY

WILLIAM WILFRID WEBB M.B

SURGEON CAPTAIN INDIAN MEDICAL SERVICE
BENGAL ARMY

Illustrated by a Map and by Twelve Plates of Coins after drawings made by the author from specimens in his collection

Westminster

ARCHIBALD CONSTABLE AND CO

PUBLISHERS TO THE INDIA OFFICE

14 PARLIAMENT STREET S·W

1893

TABLE OF CONTENTS.

LIST OF ILLUSTRATIONS.

Symbols used on the Plates.

N = gold. AR = silver. Æ = copper.

PREFACE

In my leisure time, during the years spent on duty at the Courts of Udaipur and Bíkaner, I devoted my attention to the subject of the coinage in the Native States of Rájputána. The information (derived from personal observation, from the study of my unique collection of coins of the Province, from correspondence with brother-officers serving under the Indian Foreign Office, and with many friends among the Princes and the officials at their Courts) I have during my furlough embodied into the following work, which I now venture to offer to Government as, perhaps, a more perfect representation of the questions involved than is at present possessed, and in the hope that a further consideration of the points to which I have endeavoured to call attention may be productive of good to the inhabitants of the large tract of country, the circulating mediums of which are here considered. I may add that the country in which the coins here treated of are circulating, has an area of about 126,000 square miles. In 1891 it had a population of nearly 12,000,000, and at the present rate of exchange the revenues of its Princes alone amount to over two millions sterling.

It must be evident to those who consider the matter that the subjects of the Native Princes are at present labouring under great disadvantages in regard to the currency question, when compared with the people of India who are living directly under the rule of the Queen-Empress. The following Table shows the present state of the coinage in the Hindu Princedoms of Rájputána. It will be seen that there are now circulating no less than 12 gold muhrs of different values (besides fractional gold pieces), 6 of which are now being yearly issued; 59 rupees (in most cases fractional coins to correspond), most of which are of different worths, and 16 of which are now being issued every year; and 41 different copper coins, of which 16 are struck each year, or almost every year.

The average yearly amount of issue for five recent years in the Márwár State is as follows:—of gold-muhrs, 19,757; of rupees, 311,427; and of copper coins, 175,455. These numbers for one of the richer States will allow of some idea being formed of the yearly issue of coin in Rájputána; for supposing that a proportional amount to its income be coined by each State, then the yearly issue of rupees alone amounts to considerably over two millions.

The amount of local coin circulating in the Rájput States is very large, and is, in most cases, the collection of a century or longer. I have been unable to discover that at present any systems exist for the recall of light coin. In many States coins of great age are still accepted in payment.

The coins of the Native States are fashioned in a rude way with the hammer and anvil, and have plain, unmilled edges. Stamping is carried out in a similarly rough manner — one workman holding the piece of metal between the two dies, whilst a second, with a blow from a heavy hammer, completes the coin. With very few exceptions, the coins bear only portions of the inscriptions carried by the dies.

TABLE OF COINS AT PRESENT IN CIRCULATION IN THE RÁJPUT STATES

State	Now being coined										Old coins in circulation to a considerable amount		
	Gold				Silver					Copper	Gold	Silver	Copper
	Muhrs	½ muhrs	¼ muhrs	⅛ muhrs	Rupees	8 anna	4 anna	2 anna	1 anna		Muhrs	Rupees	
Mewár . .	2				2	2	2	2	2	2		3	1
Salúmba . .										1			
Bhínda . .										1			
Sháhpura .											1	1	1
Partábgarh					1	1	1	1		1		1*	1
Dúngárpur										1			
Bánswára .					1	1	1			1			1
Márwár . .	1	1	1		1	1	1			1	2	7	3
Kúchawan					1	1	1					1	
Bíkaner . .					1	1	1	1		1		5	6
Kishangarh	1				1						1	1	
Jaipur . . .	1				1	1	1	1		1	2	2	3
Khetrí . .												1	
Búndí . . .					1					1		4	1
Kotah . . .					1	1	1	1		1		2	1
Jháláwár .					1	1	1	1		1		1	1
Alwar . . .					†							4	4
Karaulí . .					1	1	1			1		2	2
Jaisalmer .	1	1	1	1	1	1	1	1		1		1	
Bhartpur .					1	1	1	1		1		4	
Dholpur . .					1	1						3	
	6	2	2	1	16	14	13	9	2	16	6	43	25

* Several issues of this coin with different values.

† Milled rupee issued for the Mahárájá from the Calcutta mint.

Some years ago, after the institution of an enquiry into the condition of the coinage, the Government of India issued the following order: — (Foreign Department No. 402, F, dated October 6th, 1870, No. 25, Resolution 3). "His Excellency in Council thinks it right to declare that where mints have been suppressed altogether, or have not been in active use within the last five years, their revival or opening cannot be permitted." In spite of this resolution, as will be seen by examination of the following pages, mints for both silver and gold have been re-opened in some States.

In 1870 a recommendation was made, by the Agent to the Governor-General for Rájputána, to the Government of India that certain rupees then being coined in the Province should be spared, and permission given for the continuation of their issue. The ground of the recommendation was that they were much used on the occasions of marriage ceremonies; being of less value than other rupees circulating a considerable saving was thus effected, and by using them the gift or expenditure was magnified, and the good name for liberality maintained. I beg to point out that the need for the retention of these rupees no longer exists now that the amounts to be spent on marriage ceremonies have been regulated and determined upon by the Rájputs, under the guiding hand of Colonel C. K. M. Walter, C.S.I.

The composition of the coins in an issue of these States is in most cases variable. This is to be expected, as the pay of the mint officials is poor, and consequently there is a temptation to issue coins of an inferior quality to the authorised standards.

The circulation of a large number of coins of different values, and in most cases very badly stamped and rudely fashioned, re-acts in the following harmful ways:—

1. Great trouble is given to the merchants residing in Rájputána in the keeping of and in the adjustment of their accounts.

2. The question of exchange leads to continual gambling, not only amongst the merchants and bankers, but also among the native youths, for the exchange rate of the Imperial and Native currencies is continually fluctuating, due to the fraudulent schemes of the native money-lenders.

3. Distress and inconvenience fall on the agricultural and poorer classes, the members of which are continually mulcted of small sums by dishonest merchants, who represent the exchange rate as being different from that which it is in reality.

4. The multiplicity of badly executed coins facilitates the work of the coiner. As the coins of most of the Native States are very badly struck, it is a comparatively easy matter to counterfeit them, hence the amount of base coin in circulation is considerable. Even if the stamping of the pieces were to be improved upon it would not, in my opinion, much effect this evil, for the Native Chiefs will not exercise the same surveillance over their currencies as is exercised in British India to prevent the counterfeiting of the coin of the Queen-Empress. If the Imperial coins were alone current in the Native States, sufficient influence might be brought to bear on the Ráj officials to oblige the protection of the currency, and the much greater difficulty which exists in forging the Imperial milled coin would act as an additional safeguard.

5. The issue of coin by the Native Princes is a loss to the revenue of the Government of India, for were these coins suppressed an equivalent amount of Imperial coin would be required.

6. In some of the States the silver pieces are made from the

Imperial coin, which is melted down for the purpose. This practice leads to a great destruction of the Queen's currency and to its degradation. This statement would I know be indignantly denied by the native officials, but from careful enquiries which I have made through friends at the Native Courts, I can vouch for its correctness.

From the consideration of the above-mentioned circumstances, and knowing that the only Rájput States which have accepted the invitation made to the Native Princes, in the Government Resolution (Financial Department), No. 2227, dated 30th of September, 1872, are the States of Alwar and Bíkaner, in the case of each of which the issue of special coin, minted for the State at Calcutta, has been introduced during a minority, and under the orders of the British Political Agent, acting as President of the Council of Regency; knowing also the improbability of any of the Chiefs or the Councils of the States in future accepting the invitation, or of their allowing the introduction of Imperial coin, as the sole currency, except under pressure or during future minorities, I beg, with diffidence, to submit the following points with a view to opening up a discussion on the means of rectifying the existing evils:—

1. Whether the privilege of coining, at present exercised by the Native Princes, shall be indefinitely retained?

2. Whether it may not be possible to impose certain restrictions under which the continuation of the privilege can alone be exercised?

With reference to the first query, I wish to observe that if the Government desired to pass an order abolishing the privilege, no hardship could really be complained of by the Rájput Princes. For although Colonel Sutherland, Agent to the Governor-General for the States of Rájputána, wrote to the Under-Secretary to the Government of India, on the 23rd of January, 1847, as follows: "The time is yet far distant, I fear, when we can hope to make the Company's rupee the circulating medium of these Countries, for the right of coinage is, in the estimation of the Native States, one of the emblems of Sovereignty," yet I beg to submit that Colonel Sutherland magnified the importance of the point, for I have failed to discover that for centuries the ancestors of any of these Princes exercised the power of coining. No coins can now be produced which can with certainty be accredited to any of the existing Native States between the 12th and the end of the 17th or beginning of the 18th century (Mewár excepted). Certainly from the days of the Mughal supremacy the power of coining, if it were then being exercised, was taken away. The present mints only date from the decline of the Muhammadan power, and the practice of coining was only assumed in consequence of the weakness of the suzerain at Dehlí, and in most cases for the purpose of making revenue by the circulation of debased coin, which was supported at an enhanced nominal value through the introduction of the purer standards of neighbouring districts. When the present mints were opened sanads of permission were obtained by purchase or extortion from the Dehlí Court, and the Princes placed on their coins the Emperor's name and superscription as a titular avowal of Dehlí supremacy.

As regards the second query, it appears to me that if the continuation of coining be permitted indefinitely, one of the following methods of procedure may perhaps be arranged:—

1. That the Imperial Government coins be issued for each State from the Calcutta or Bombay mint, under the regulations laid

down in the Despatch No. 2227 from the Government of India in the Financial Department, dated Simla, 30th of September, 1872.

2. That the Imperial Government provide dies and machinery for the coining of money for each Native State (charging the actual cost of the dies and machinery), and give distinct orders as to the purity and weight of the coins to be issued, providing trained mint-officers for the service of the Durbars, and making the Political Officers accredited to the Courts responsible to see that the orders of Government be duly observed and carried out. This latter would be an expensive if a workable way of getting over the difficulty, and I believe that if the matter were laid before the different Native Princes, and the necessity of a uniformity in the coinage again demonstrated, a number of them would without further trouble accede to the offer made to them by Government in the Despatch above quoted from.

I desire to offer my best thanks to Professor Cecil Bendall, M.A., to Mr. E. J. Rapson, M.A., and Mr. H. A. Grueber, F.S.A., the former of the Department of Oriental MSS., and the two latter of the Coin Department in the British Museum, for their kindness in revising the proofs and for many valuable suggestions, and also to Mr. Archibald Constable for thoughtful help and for the great care which he has taken in bringing out this monograph. It is also a pleasant duty to render thanks to Sir Joseph Fayrer, K.C.S.I., Sir George Birdwood, K.C.I.E., Colonel P. W. Powlett, C.S.I., Captain C. Herbert, and to many friends, European and Native, dwelling in Rájputána for the aid and support which they have given to me. I wish also to acknowledge my indebtedness to many works on Indian history and antiquities which have been consulted and made use of during the preparation of this volume, and especially to James Prinsep's

"Essays on Indian Antiquities," edited by Edward Thomas; Lieutenant-Colonel James Tod's "Annals and Antiquities of Rajast'hán"; "The Gazetteer of India," by Sir W. W. Hunter, K.C.S.I., C.I.E.; Colonel G. B. Malleson's "Historical Sketch of the Native States of India," and to Mr. Stanley Lane-Poole's works—"The Coins of the Sultáns of Dehlí," and "The Coins of the Muhammadan States of India."

WILLIAM WILFRID WEBB,
SURGEON CAPTAIN,
BENGAL ARMY.

2, PROBY SQUARE,
BLACKROCK, DUBLIN,
May 10th, 1893.

INDEX

MEWÁR CURRENCIES

MEWÁR PLATE I

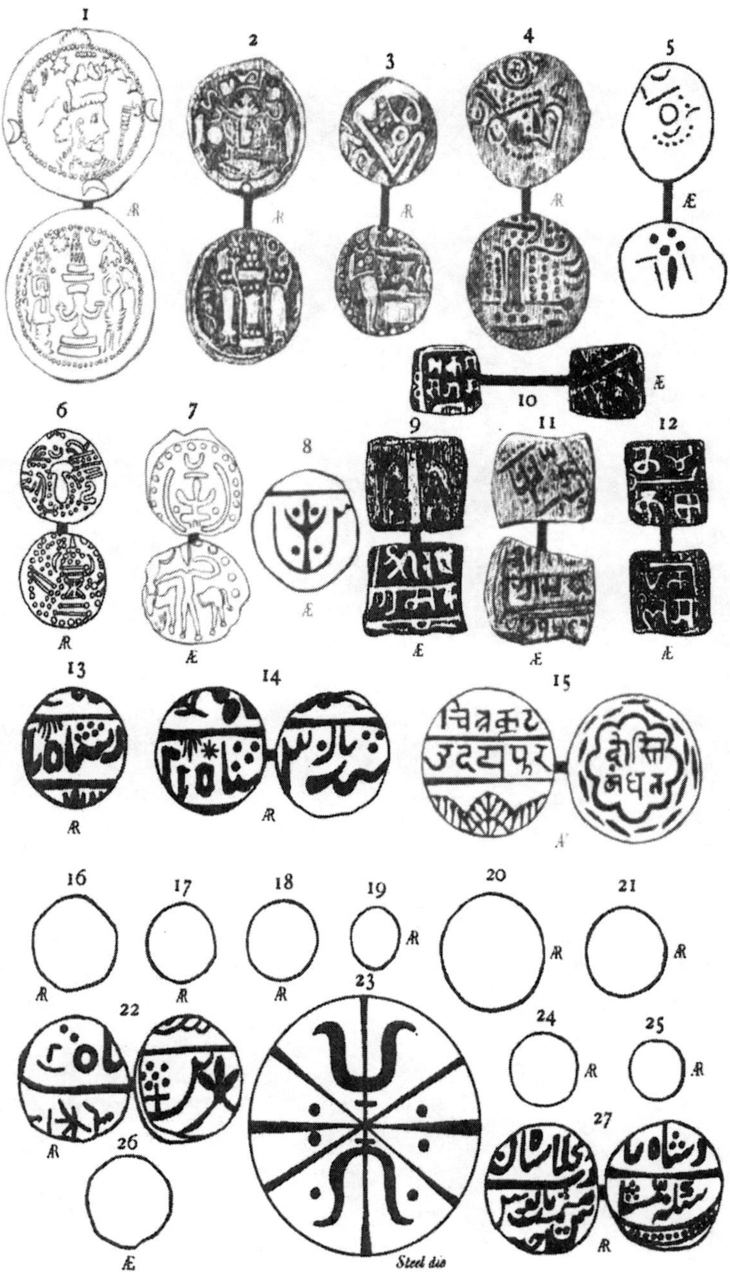

MEWÁR

MODERN CAPITAL UDAIPUR. ANCIENT CAPITAL CHITOR (CHITRAKUṬA)

The area of Mewár (Meváḍ) is 12,861 square miles, the population in 1891, was 1,862,478 or 145 persons per square mile. The revenue is about £510,000 a year, of which £180,000 belongs to the Chief.

The Maháráná of Udaipur is the representative of the most ancient ruling race in the world, whether in the east or the west. Whatever may be the true origin of the family, whether the descent from Ráma or that from the Sassanian Kings of Persia be the true one, will probably never be settled, but we have absolute historic proof that the Mahárána's ancestors were settled as kings in Saurāshtra—the country of the Sauras or "Sun-worshippers"—in the 2nd century of our era. In Saurāshtra their capital was Vallabhípura, and thence, after its sack in the 6th century, Pushpavatí, one of the Queens of Síláditya, the last prince of the house to rule in the peninsula, fled to Edur. After her flight the Queen gave birth to a son who was called "Goha" or "cave-born," and who was given the country of Edur by the Bhíls. His name became the patronymic of his descendants, who were called "Gohilote," in time softened into "Gehlot." The 8th prince of the family who ruled over Edur lost his kingdom, and his infant son "Bappa," was removed to the wilds of Parassur. Bappa took Chitor from the Mori prince of the Prámar race, then paramount sovereign of Hindústán, in A.D. 728. Until nearly the middle of the 16th century Chitor remained the capital of Mewár, but at that time, in the reign of Udaya-Siṇha, it fell into the hands of Akbar, after a gallant defence. Later on Udaya-Siṇha, founded Udaipur, the present capital. For the next two centuries and a half the country and the princes of Mewár were continually in trouble, first of all from the determination of the Muhammadans to reduce this ancient house to a condition of vassalage, and afterwards from the rapacity of the Maráthás; but in spite of all their sufferings, and though obliged to admit the supremacy of the Mughals, the Udaipur House always, to a certain extent, preserved its independence, and it was the only one in Rájputána which never gave a daughter to share the marriage couch of the Muhammadan Emperor of Dehlí. In 1817 the treaty with the British was signed, since which date peace has reigned in the country, and prosperity has gradually returned both to princes and people.

The ancient title of the princes was "Ráwul," which was changed to that of "Rāná," in consequence of the victorious issue of a contest with the Purihara prince of Mundore, who bore that of "Rāná," and who surrendered it with his life and capital to the Mewár Chief.

On migration from the wilds of Edur to Ahár, an ancient city close to the modern capital, the name of the family was changed from "Gehlote" to "Ahária" (the name still borne by the Princes of Dúngarpur), by which the race continued to be designated until the 12th century, when the name "Sesodiá" was adopted.

Of the ancient coins of this kingdom very little is known. That coins were issued by the princes prior to the invasion of Akbar is certain, and some of them are now recognizable with tolerable certitude, but for the most part the question as to what coins were current in the State prior to the 16th century, and as to what dynasties many of the coins found in the country are attributable, is a mere matter of conjecture. After the conquest of Akbar and up to the time when the Chitor mint was re-opened, no doubt the coins of Muhammadan conquerors were chiefly used.

Without question the class of coins known as the "Indo-Sassanian" (see Plate I. figs. 2, 3, 4, 5, and 6), were for a long period the chief currency. These coins are the descendants of the Sassanian type coined in Persia, a specimen of which is depicted by fig. 1 of the same plate. The Indo-Sassanian coins are found in pretty pure silver, in copper, and in a mixture of the metals in various proportions. They are found in very large numbers in Mewár, and the copper specimens of the issue, in its most debased form, are still in circulation in the bázárs. I have obtained specimens of this coinage in many parts of Mewár during my travels, and have had specimens brought to me which have been dug up in many parts of the State. Some years ago there was a great find of these coins at Chandimpura, the finest examples from which are now in my Cabinet. The most debased of these coins go by the name of *Phadias* (?), they are said to have been largely in circulation some three or four hundred years ago, or about the time of Akbar's invasion, and I think that this is not improbable, for a number of these debased coins were brought to me having been dug up in the Kothyan fort, in Sháhpura territory, a fort of no great age; this fact would support the tradition that these coins formed part of the cir culating medium at no very distant date. Fig. 6 is a Gadhia coin. These coins are very common in Mewár, and are found in silver and copper. Copper specimens can be found in almost any old bázár, and a few years back a large earthen pot of silver coins was found at the foot of the Chitor hill, some of which I now possess. Many of these coins are also found at Ahár, an ancient capital of the Maháráná's family before the conquest of Chitor in A.D 728. On some of the Gadhia coins the Sassanian fire-altar is replaced by an inscription in Devanágarí. My correspondent, the late Bhagwánlál Indraji, considered the latter to belong to Gujarát; I have found them at Chitor, but my specimens are not in sufficient number to obtain any clear readings.

These coins of the Sassanian type go to support the theory of the Persian descent of the Maháráná of Udaipur. The type may have been brought to Mewár when the family fled from Sauráshtra, and as time passed by and the meaning of the symbols was forgotten the issue became more and more debased. The gadhia type of coin is supposed to be as old as the 5th century. The gadhia may be the coin of the Persian monarch Bahrám, struck in India, which would account for the poorness of the execution. The words "Gor" and "Gadha" have the same signification, meaning the "wild-ass," and are surnames for Bahrám, given in consequence of his partiality to hunting that animal. Various authorities state that Bahrám was in India in the fifth century, and that he left offspring there; Major Tod makes mention of a prince named "Gardhabhela" as ruling at Vallabhípura, and says that it had been surmised that he was the son of Bahrám (Byrámgor), and the Maháráná's true ancestor. The issue of the gadhia coins must have been continued over many centuries. The obverse side of the Indo-Sassanian coins has the king's head to the left, with fragments of inscription which appear to be in Pehlví character; the reverse side shows the Sassanian fire-altar. As will be subsequently seen I consider the Dhinglá paisa (see Plate II. fig. 8), which is now current in the State to be the descendant of the Indo-Sassanian coins. The Indo-Sassanian coins are of course not confined to Mewár, but from the large numbers dug up in the State it is evident that they were at one time the coins of the country.

The earliest coins which are attributed to a Mewár ruler by name are those said to have been struck by Ráwul Guhil, son of Bappa Ráwul and the founder of the Gehlot dynasty. Guhil ascended the throne of Chitor in A.D. 753. The coin has been alluded to by Major-General Cunningham in the 4th volume of his *Archæological Reports*, pp. 95 and 96. In the year 1869 upwards of two thousand of these small silver coins were dug up at Agra. They bear, in an ancient western form of the Sanskrit character, the inscription "Srí Guhila." Carlleyle attributed these coins to Guhila (remarking that he may have held sway over Agra), or to Goha, son of Sïláditya, the first of the Gehlot branch of the expelled dynasty of Vallabhípura.

The copper "Bull and Horseman" series of coins (Chohán Horseman and Bull, Nandí) were at one time attributed to Rahap, the 39th ruler, and to Hammíra, the 52nd ruler, but these coins are now known to belong to other dynasties, and not one of them can be attributed to a Mewár Ráná. The type from which these coins were struck can be seen at Plate IV. fig. 4 (Samanta Deva), and one of the coins formerly attributed to a Mewár Chief at fig. 6 of the same plate.

Ráná Khumbo, who succeeded to the gaddí in A.D. 1418, and reigned until 1468, coined *tangkas* in his own name, and he is reported to have presented some of them to Mahmúd Khán of Málwáh (Sultán Mahmúd Khiljí) in 1450.

General Cunningham possesses two specimens of Khumbo's issue, which he obtained from Stacy's collection. Both the coins are square and of copper, they are of different weights. The dates on the coins are Samvat, 1510 and 1523.

In A.D. 1509 Mahárání Sangrám Siṇha came to the gaddí, and reigned until A.D. 1528. He issued a coin which is described on pp. 297–298, Vol. I. of Prinsep's *Essays on Indian Antiquities*, edited by Thomas (London, Murray, 1858). These coins are rare; I have only been able to collect four copper specimens

Obverse. "Srí Sangrám Siṇha, and the date 1580." (Samvat 1580.)

श्री {संग्राम / संग्रम / संग्रम} सिंह १५८० — Sangrám appears to be written in three ways on the coins.

Reverse. An attempt at a human figure formed with curved lines? The word "Sháh" in the Persian character is pretty clear on some specimens, and a heart-shaped sign and the Trisúl are generally present.

Weight. About 126 grains.

See Plate I. figs. 9, 10, 11, and 12.

The greater number of the existing coins bear the date S. 1575, those of S. 1580 are very rare. The coins, like the copper issues of Malwah of the same period, are of two different weights. General Sir A. Cunningham possesses five specimens. The inscription varies. On the obverse the inscription is either "Srí Sangrám sah," "Ráná Sangram Sah," or "Srí Ráná Sangrám sah" (Sah for Siṇha). On the reverses of Cunningham's coins there are a few rough Persian letters, one of the coins bears the Swastika emblem.

In General Sir A. Cunningham's cabinet there are two specimens of the coinage of Ráná Vikramáditya, and four specimens of that of Baṇbír, of Tod, and Prinsep (probably Vaṇavíra, the coins read वव, but they are all rude and imperfect, they also give १५ for the hundreds in the date). Those of Vikramáditya (A.D. 1532-35) are of different weights, on the obverse the legend "Ráná Srí Vikramáditya" and the date are found in Nágari, on the reverse the word "Sultán" can be recognized in Persian character. The coins of Baṇbír are all of the same weight, and are of the larger, heavier variety; they bear the inscription "Srí ráná Vaṇavíra"?.

The larger coins of these Chiefs, like those of Sangrám Singh, are "copper" or "black tangkas" (pana). The weight of the black tangka was 80 ratis of 1.8 grains each, or 144 grains, the exchange rate was 50 to the rupee.

There is a coin which, although not struck by a Rájput chief, must not be omitted in a description of the coins of Mewár. I refer to the rupee which Akbar the Great struck at Chitor. Akbar laid siege to the fort on the 19th Rabiussani, A.H. 975 (23rd October, 1567), and it fell into his hands and was sacked on the 25th Shabán (Tuesday, 24th Feb. 1568). After the sack the Conqueror struck a coin in the old capital of Mewár, and stamped on it the letters गा ("GA´")[1] which are said to refer to the proverb "Gao máryá rá páp"—a proverb which had its origin in the slaughter at Chitor.

The coin depicted on Plate II. fig. 15, was presented to me at Chitor as a specimen of this issue, but from its style and inscription it is evidently of later date. It is probably a local coin struck in the name of Akbar 2nd.

INSCRIPTION.

Obverse. سکه مبارک بادشاه غازي اکبر شاه
Sikka mubárak bádsháh ghází Akbar Sháh.

Reverse. ضرب سنة ۱۴ جلوس میمنت مانوس गा
Zarab sanah 14 *julús maimanat mánús GA´*

Symbols. . Weight. 176 grains.

THE MINT

Three State mints have been worked in Mewár—at Chitor, Udaipur, and Bhílwárrá.

The Chitor mint is said to have been opened on the conclusion of the treaty between Mahárána Amar Sinha 1st, and the Emperor Jehángir, in A.D. 1615 (S. 1671-2). It is stated by Kavirájá Shyamál Dás, that the Mahárána obtained permission to issue a coin called after his own capital, but bearing the Emperor's name in Persian characters. As will be seen, when detailing what is known of the Chitorí coins, no specimens earlier than those of the time of the Emperor Sháh A´lam are procurable, nor can I find any mention of the existence of such coins. It is possible that the permission to coin was obtained at the time Kavirájá states, but that the power was not made use of, or only to a very limited extent.

Permission for the opening of the Udaipur mint was obtained in S. 1770 (A.D. 1714), by Pancholi Bihári Dás, a Kayath Prime Minister to Mahárána Sangrám Sinha 2nd, who was sent to the Court of the Emperor Farukshir for the purpose. I do not, however, believe that any coins were struck at this mint until the days of Sháh 'A´lam.

[1] This coin is referred to by Prinsep, p. 68, Useful Tables, London, 1858.

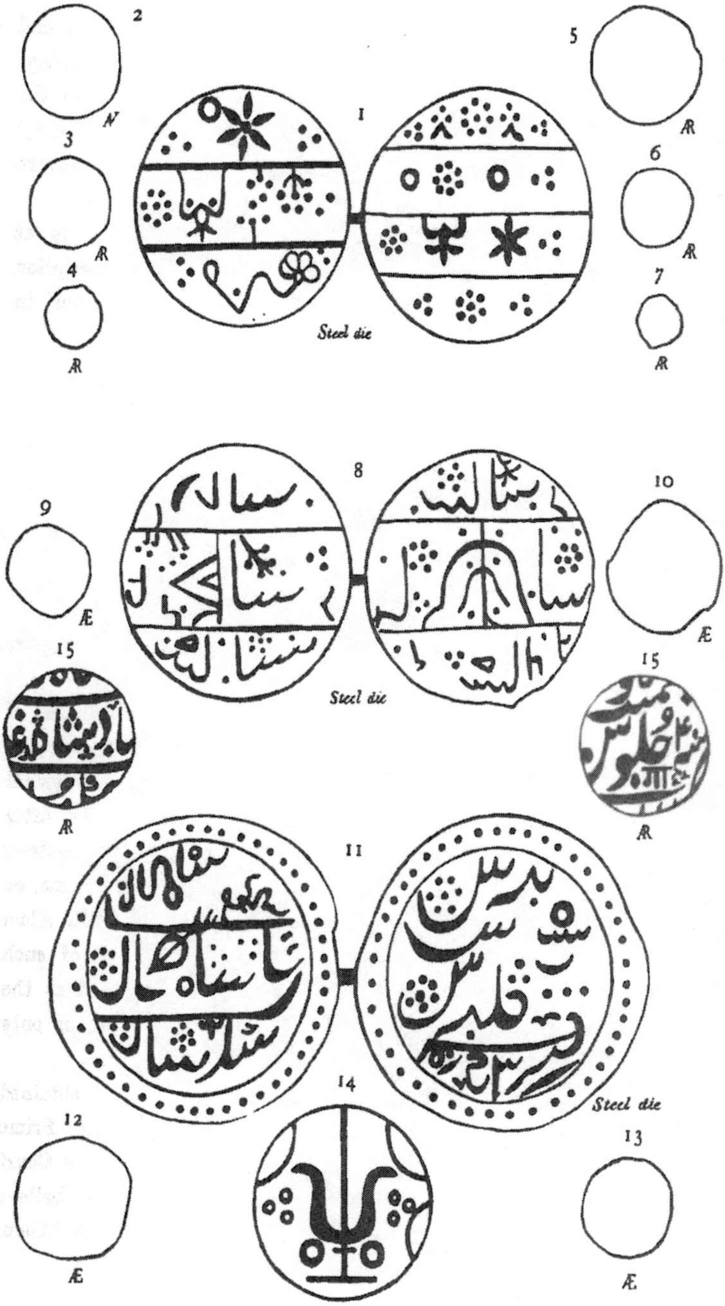

1
2
3
4
5
6
7
8
9
10
11
12
13
14
15
15
Steel die
Steel die
Steel die
Steel die

If earlier coins do or did exist I have not seen them, though I have made diligent search.

No records exist to show when the Bhílwárrá mint was first worked, but doubtless it was in the days of Sháh Álam. Bhílwárrá was at one time one of the greatest marts in Rájputána, but at the early part of this century it was deserted and in ruins. Tod had it rebuilt. It is now a place of commercial importance.

Mint marks given by Prinsep (*Useful Tables*, Pl. xlvi.), but not to be found on the coins described in this work.

Udaipur.

Chitor.

Bhílwárrá.

GOLD COINAGE

1. The Chandorí Muhr. These coins have only been minted at Udaipur, and are still issued. They were first struck by Maháráná Swarúp Siṇha between the years 1842 and 1861. The pieces bear the same symbols as the other Chandorí coins of the second issue. See Plate II. figs. 1 and 2, the latter for the size of an average coin.

Weight. 7 máshas, or about 116 grains.

Assay. 3½ máshas and 1 rattí of gold, 2¾ máshas and 1 rattí of silver, and ½ a másha of copper.

2. The Swarúp Sháhí Muhr. This piece was first struck in A.D. 1851-2 (S. 1908) and is still issued. It was formerly made at Chitor as well as at Udaipur, but is now only issued from the latter mint. See Plate I. fig. 15.

INSCRIPTION.

Obverse. चित्रकूट उदयपुर

Chitrakúta Udayapur. A line between the words, and another below the inscription, the latter separating it from some symbols said to represent the hills of Mewár.

Reverse. दोस्ति लंधन

Dosti Londhon, "Friend of London," within a border of eight scollops, outside which are two circles each formed by seven broken segments. The form Chitrakúta is the Sanskrit original of the modern Chitor, "kuta" signifying mountain.

Weight—169 grains. The gold is said to be pure.

SILVER COINAGE

It is asserted that the tin mines of Mewár were once very productive, yielding no inconsiderable amount of the silver used in the coinage. Political reasons, during the Mughal domination, led to the concealment of such sources of wealth. The caste of miners has long been extinct.

1. The Chitorí coins. See Plate I. fig. 13. Permission to issue these coins is said to have been obtained in A.D. 1615, but it is most probable that they were first issued in the time of the Emperor Sháh 'Álam (A.D. 1707-1712). The pieces are the rupee, eight-anna, and four-anna bits. The Chitor mint has been closed for some years now.

INSCRIPTION.

Obverse. سکه مبارک بادشاه غازي شاه عالم

Sikka mubárak bádsháh ghází Sháh 'Álam.

"The auspicious coin of the victorious Emperor Sháh 'Álam."

Symbols—5 strokes over the "h" of "Bádsháh."

Reverse. سنة جلوس میمنت مانوس

Sanah julús maimanat mánús.

"In the year of his fortunate reign."

Value, 12½ annas Imperial and one or two Dhinglás given in. Prinsep gives the value of 100 coins at 82 004 kull-dár coins, the weight at 169.57 grains, and the pure contents at 135.31 grains. When Tod wrote his Rájást'hán he said, "The Chitor rupee is now 31 per cent. inferior to the old Bhílárá (Bhílwárrá) standard."

2. The Udaipur coins. See Plate I. fig. 14, and for the sizes of the smaller pieces figs. 16, 17, 18, and 19. The coins are the rupee, eight-anna, four-anna, two-anna, and one-anna pieces. They were first struck by Mahárána Sangrám Siṇha II., who occupied the gaddí of Mewár from A.D. 1711 to 1734, and were issued until Swarúp Siṇha introduced his new coin. The Udaipur rupee is the standard coin of

the country, and all Durbár payments are made in it or its equivalents. The three smaller pieces are rare.

INSCRIPTION.

Obverse. The same as in No. 1.

Symbols. A jhár of six branches, a star of five or eight points over the final "h" in "bádsháh," five lines depending from the "í" of "ghází," a circle of dots with a central one within the "í" of "ghází."

Reverse. ضرب ودیپور سنه جلوس میمنت مانوس

Zarab Udaipur sanah julús maimanat mánús.

"Struck at Udaipur in the year of his fortunate reign."

Value. 12¼ annas Imperial.

In Prinsep's *Useful Tables*, (p. 58) the weight is given at 167.45 grains, the pure contents at 130.82 grains, and the value of 100 is put down at 79.285 kull-dár coins.

3. Bhím Siṇha's Chandorí coins. See Plate I. fig. 22. These coins were named after Chand Kunwar Baí, sister to Bhím Siṇha. The princess never married, she lived and died in the Udaipur palace. It is said that Bhím Siṇha gave away so much in charity that his sister, who helped him in the management of his affairs, persuaded him to issue these coins of less value than the Chitorí and Udaipurí (then the only coins current in the State), hoping thereby to diminish the expenditure. Bhím Siṇha reigned from A.D. 1778 to 1828, and the Chandorí coins were issued in the early part of the present century. They were current during the remainder of the reign, and during the reigns of his successors, Jawán Siṇha and Sirdár Siṇha The coins of this issue are now very rarely met with, as most of them were melted down by Swarúp Siṇha when he issued the new Chandorí coin. The coins were made at the Udaipur mint only.

INSCRIPTION.

Obverse. As in No. 1. Symbol. A badly stamped jhár.

Reverse. As in No. 1. The Persian character is very badly executed.

Symbols. Circles of dots in the "S" of "Julús," a figure like, in some respects, to the one on Swarúp Siṇha's Chandorí coins.

Weight. 168 grains.

4. Swarúp Siṇha's Chandorí coins. See Plate II. fig. 1, and for the sizes of the coins figs. 3, 4, 5, 6, and 7. These coins were first issued by Swarúp Siṇha between the years 1842 and 1861, they are still regularly coined. They have always been made at the Udaipur mint. As Swarúp Siṇha considered it to be improper to use coins bearing a Persian inscription as gifts to Brahmins and Bards and for other religious purposes, he called in Bhím Siṇha's Chandorí coins, and melting them down struck the new Chandorí coins. It is said that the symbols on the dies are without signification, the pattern is reported to have been drawn by the Maháráná at a Durbár.

The coins are the rupee, eight-anna, four-anna, two-anna, and one-anna pieces. The pieces are all stamped from the same die, the smaller bits receiving a very small portion of the pattern.

Description. See fig. 1 Plate II. which is taken from the die at the mint.

Weight. The rupee 168 grains, and the smaller pieces in exact proportion.

Value. The rupee is stated to be worth 9 annas, 9 pies, and 2 pice Imperial, three-fourths of the value of the Udaipur coin (12¾ annas Udaipur).

Assay. The composition of both the issues of Chandorí coins is said to be 6 parts of silver and 2 parts of copper.

The Chandorí silver pieces are as a rule very badly stamped, some of the dies from which coins have been struck bear symbols of a finer cut than those found upon others.

5. The Swarúp Sháhi coins. The pieces are the rupee, eight-anna, four-anna, two-anna, and one-anna bits. Each coin bears the full inscription, but the smaller pieces want the outer circles of lines on the reverse. See Plate I. fig. 15 (but in silver), and for the sizes of the smaller coins figs. 20, 21, 24, and 25. For a description see under gold coinage, No. 2. Value, 13½ annas Imperial.

6. The Bhílwárrá Rupee. There are no records to show when this piece was first minted, it bears an inscription to Sháh 'Álam, and is one of the coins mentioned by Mr. Wilder as being current in the Ajmere District in A.D. 1819. The coining of this piece was discontinued prior to the year 1870. The coin is current about Bhílwárrá, in the

Bhíl country of Mewár, and is largely in circulation amongst the Bhíl and Grassia tribes in Sirohí. (Sirohí is a State ruled over by the Deora princes, a branch of the Chohans.) From a letter addressed by Capt. Baylay to the Agent to the Governor-General in 1870, I learn that the Bhílwárrá rupee of Mewár is said to have been first struck in the days of Sháh Jahán; but the correctness of this statement is much open to doubt. When Baylay wrote, 100 Bhílwárrá rupees were worth 91 rupees and 12 annas Imperial. See Plate I. fig. 27.

INSCRIPTION.

Obverse. As in No. I. Symbol. The jhar.

Reverse. ضرب دار الخلافة شاه جهان آباد سنة جلوس میمنت مانوس

Zarab dár al Khilafah Sháh Jahánábád sanah julús maimanat mánús.

"Minted at the seat of the Khilafah Dehlí, in the year of his fortunate reign."

Weight The weight of some of the coins is 170 grains, but the Calcutta Tables give the weight 168.90 grains.

Value. The value is Rs. 1. 2*a.* 6*p.* Udaipurí. According to the Calcutta Tables 100 of the coins are equal to 84.663 Imperial Rs.

COPPER COINAGE

There are three copper coins current in Mewár under the sanction of the Durbár—the "Trisúlia," the "Dhinglá," and the "Bhílwárrá."

1. The Dhinglá paisá. The date of the introduction of this coin is unknown. The Durbár authorities say that it is a coin of great antiquity, and I can well believe this, for I think it is a descendant of the old Sassanian type, and that it still bears "the fire-altar" on its reverse side. The reverses of figs. 1, 2, 3, 4, 5, 6, and 7 (Plate I.), show the Sassanian fire-altar; fig. 8 of the same Plate the reverse of an old "Dhinglá," which bears a figure which I believe to be a still further degraded form of this ancient emblem. Fig. 7, derived from the Indo-Scythic coins of Vasudeva, shows a figure much like that seen on the Dhinglá, but Mr. E. J. Rapson thinks that this represents a debasement of the standing figure of the king and not of the fire-altar, and according to this view the figure in the plate is upside down. The whole of the symbols on the die of the coin (at present being issued) can be seen at Pl. II. fig. 8, where it will be noticed that what I take to be the inverted fire-

altar is mixed up with hieroglyphics which may be attempts at Persian words. Figs. 9 and 10 of the same Plate show the sizes of large and small specimens of the variety. This coin is still issued. The coins are not made at the Durbár mint, but the Sonárs (goldsmiths) at Umarda, a village three kos from Udaipur, have the monopoly of the coinage, paying a yearly sum to the Durbár for the exclusive right. In old days the coins were issued from the Udaipur mint, and at a visit I paid to the mint in the year 1887, I saw some of the old dies formerly in use.

Weight. Prinsep in his *Useful Tables*, p. 63, mentions that the Mewár copper coin weighed 34 grains. I have specimens in my collection weighing from 43 to 100 grains; the present coins are of about the former weight.

2. The "Trisúlia" (adapted from the trident—trisúl—of Siva) or "Mewár" paisá. See Plate I. fig. 23 for the obverse, fig. 26 for the size of an average coin, and Plate II. fig. 14 for the reverse. The drawings of the surfaces are from the dies. The coins are made by the Sonárs of Chitor, who have the monopoly. The coin is chiefly used by the people living in the tract of country between Akolá and Chitor. It is believed to be even a more ancient coin than the Dhinglá paisá. Some specimens in circulation want the cross-bars near the centre on the obverse (see fig. 23), and the circles or dots, arranged in threes, on the reverse (see fig. 14).

Weight. About 85 grains. Value. 2 pice.

3. The old Bhílwárrá paisá. This was probably coined about the same time as the rupee. It bears the same inscription, see silver coins, No. 6.

Symbols. The lotus depending from the "í" of "ghází," and the "trident" above "mubárak" (?), on the obverse.

Weight. There are several coins of different sizes and weights in circulation which were all made at Bhílwárrá and bear the same inscription. I have specimens weighing from 86 to 65 grains, which are evidently a distinct issue (as far as value is concerned) from the ordinary old Bhílwárrá paisá, which weighs about 273 grains. Prinsep (*Tables*, p. 62) states the weight to be 307 grains.

4. The more modern Bhílwárrá paisá. See Plate II. fig. 11, and fig. 12 for the size of an average coin. It is not known when this coin was first issued, and no specimens have been struck for many years. The coin is current about Mándalguṛh, Jeházepur, and Bhílwárrá.

INSCRIPTION.

Obverse. سکہ مبارک بادشاہ غازي محمد شاہ بہادر

Sikka mubárak bádsháh ghází Muhammad Sháh bahádur.

"Auspicious coin of the victorious Emperor Muhammad Sháh."

Symbols. The lotus, circles of dots.

Reverse. ضرب سنہ ٥ جلوس میمنت مانوس

Zarab . . . . . sanah 5 julús maimanat mánús

"Struck in the fifth year of his fortunate reign."

Weight. 255 grains.

Value. Of the same value as six Udaipur paisá.

LIST OF THE CHIEFS OF MEWAR FROM A.D. 1437 TO DATE.

Name	Date of ascending gaddi	Date of death	Name	Date of ascending gaddi	Date of death
1. Kumbha Karan	1437	1469	15. Sangrám Siṇha ii.	1711	1734
2. Udaya Siṇha i.	1469	1474	16. Jagat Siṇha ii.	1734	1752
3. Rai Mal	1474	1509	17. Pratáp Siṇha ii.	1752	1754
4. Sangrám Siṇha i.	1509	1527	18. Ráj Siṇha ii.	1754	1761
5. Ratan Siṇha ii.	1527	1532	19. Ari Siṇha iii.	1761	1773
6. Vikramáditya	1532	1535	20. Hammir[1] Siṇha ii	1773	1778
7. Udaya Siṇha ii.	1537	1572	21. Bhím Siṇha ii.	1778	1828
8. Pratáp Siṇha i.	1572	1597	22. Jawán Siṇha	1828	1838
9. Amar Siṇha	1597	1620	23. Sirdár Siṇha	1838	1842
10. Karan Siṇha ii	1620	1628	24. Swarúp Siṇha	1842	1861
11. Jagat Siṇha i.	1628	1652	25. Shambhú Siṇha	1861	1874
12. Ráj Siṇha i.	1652	1680	26. Sajjan Siṇha	1874	1884
13. Jai Siṇha	1680	1699	27. H H. Fatteh Siṇha, G.C.S.I.	1884	now reigning.
14. Amar Siṇha ii.	1699	1711			

A list of the earlier Chiefs will be found in Prinsep's *Useful Tables*, p. 256.

[1] Ammír.

MEWA'R FEUDATORIES

Three of the great Feudatories of Mewár have coined money. The Salúmba Ráwul, the Bhínda Ráwul, and the Rájádhirája of Sháhpúra. The latter is not only a vassal of Mewár, but also holds part of his estates directly under the British Government in the same way ás other Rájput Chiefs do. The two former, as vassals of Mewár, have exercised the power of coining without the sanction of the Durbár.

SALU'MBA

The Salúmba Chief is the head of the clan "Chondawut," he descends from Chondrá, the eldest son of Lakha Ráná (succeeded as Ráná of Mewár A.D. 1373), who renounced his birthright in favour of his younger brother, reserving as the recompense of his renunciation the first place in the Council, and stipulating that in all grants, his symbol (the "bhálá" or lance) should be superadded to the autograph of the Prince. The estate of the Salúmba Chief lies in the Hill-country between the great Dhebar lake and the Dúngarpur territory. The rent-roll is reported to be about Rs. 84,000 a year. Copper of a very fine description is found on the estate, and from it the Chief has manufactured the Padam Sahí paisá.

The Padam Sahí coin was first struck by Padam (Padma) Siṇgh, Ráwul of Salúmba from A.D. 1804 to 1848. It is also called the "Salúmba Dhinglá." It was issued until the year 1870, when the British Government ordered that the mint should be closed.

INSCRIPTION.

The obverse bears a sword, the lance, a star and a jháṛ, also the head of an arrow with some attempts at an inscription. The reverse bears some lines, an attempt at an inscription, I think part of *sanah julús maimanat mánús*. See Plate III. fig. 1.

Weight. 84 grains. Value, 2 pice.

BHI'NDA

The Bhínda Chief is the head of the Suktawut clan. He descends from Suktá, the second son of Ráná Udaya Siṇha, who ascended the

MEWÁR

SALÚMBA BHÍNDA

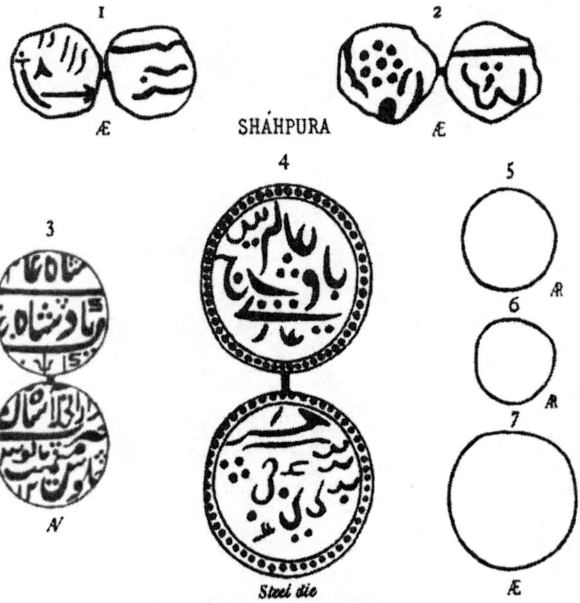

DÚNGARPUR PARTÁBGARH

gaddí of Mewár in A.D. 1537. The coin issued by this Ráwul is known as the "Bhíndrya paisá." It was first issued by Maháráj Zoráwer Siṇha, the grandfather of the present Chief who occupied the Bhínda gaddí from A.D. 1799 to 1827. On the obverse of this coin is what I take to be a rudely executed seated female figure, like that on the Ráhtore coins of Kanauj (see Plate IV. figs. 1 and 5), on the reverse the word *sháh* can be deciphered, in Persian characters. The marks on the obverse may be only some attempts at Persian characters, but the pattern is very like that on the Kanauj coins.

Weight, 132 grains. Value, 4 pice. See Plate III. fig. 2.

SHÁHPURA

The Sháhpura Chief holds two estates, together of the annual value of some £28,000. The one is in the Mándalgarh District of Mewár, and was a gift to his ancestors from a Mewár Ráná; the other was a grant from one of the Dehlí Emperors, is in the Ajmere district, and is now held direct from the British Government by payment of an annual tribute. For his estate in Mewár the Chief pays no relief, and is exempt from all but personal service at the Maháráná's court, and the local duties of the district in which his estate is situated. The Rájádhiráj of Sháhpura, for such is the Chief's title, is of the Mewár blood-royal—a Ránáwut, descended from Ráná Amar Siṇha.

The area of the Sháhpura estate is 406 square miles. In 1891 the population was 63,646, or 157 persons per square mile.

LIST OF THE SHÁHPÚRA CHIEFS

1. Súraj Mal.
2. Sajjan Siṇha.
3. Daulat Siṇha.
4. Bhárat Siṇha.
5. Ummed Siṇha.
6. Ráná Siṇha.
7. Bhím Siṇha.
8. Amar Siṇha.
9. Madho Siṇha.
10. Jagat Siṇha.
11. Lachman Siṇha.
12. Nahar Siṇha.

THE MINT

Gold, silver, and copper have all been coined at Sháhpura. The Emperor Bahádur Sháh, Sháh Álam, gave the title of Rájá to Bhárat

Singhjí about the year 1707 (1707–1710). Nahar Siṇha, the present Chief, tells me that the right of coining money was conceded to his ancestor by the Emperor together with the other honours enjoyed by the other Rájput Princes, and that gold, silver, and copper were regularly minted at Sháhpura from about 1710 to the year 1870, when the British Government passed the resolution (Foreign Department, No. 402 F, dated October 6th, 1870, No. 25, Resolution 5) directing that the mint should be closed, as the political importance of the Sháhpura State was not such as to entitle it to the privilege of an independent coinage.

The present Chief is under a wrong impression as to the date when the mint was first opened. I am pretty certain that no coins were made at Sháhpura until after the year A.D. 1785, at least I have not been able to discover any of an earlier date; my friend, Kavirájá Shyamál Dás of Udaipur, tells me he thinks the Sháhpura coins were first struck by Rájá Ummed Siṇha in A.D. 1760. Ummed Siṇha took the gaddí from his father in A.D. 1728; he fell in battle in A.D. 1768.

The gold and silver coins are known as the "Gyársanah" or "Igáráhsanah."

GOLD COINAGE

The gold muhr is very badly struck, and is of very base metal. See Plate III. fig. 3.

Obverse. سکه مبارک بادشاه غازي شاه عالم

Sikha mubárak bádsháh ghází Sháh 'Álam

"Auspicious coin of the victorious Emperor Sháh 'Álam."

Symbol. A trident over "mubárak."

Reverse. ضرب سنة جلوس میمنت مانوس دار الخلافة شاه جهان اباد ۱۲۰۰

Zarab sanah julús maimanat mánús dár al Khiláfah Sháh Jahánábád (sanah 12 or 1,200 ?).

"Minted at Dehlí the seat of the Khiláfah in the 12th year of his fortunate reign" (or, apparently, on some specimens "in the year 1200").

Weight. Supposed to be 162 grains, but I have a specimen which weighs as little as 150 grains.

SILVER COINAGE

The silver coins are the rupee, eight-anna, and four-anna pieces. See Plate III. fig. 3 (but in silver), and for the sizes of the smaller pieces, figs. 5 and 6. The inscription on these coins is the same as on the gold muhr.

Weight. Of the rupee 168-170 grains, and of the smaller coins in an exact proportion.

Assay. The rupees are said to contain 7 máshas of silver.

Value. About 10 annas Imperial.

COPPER COINAGE

The copper coins are called the Mádho Sháhí. They are named after Rájádhiráj Mádho Siṇha, the great-grandfather of the present Chief, and were struck during the time he occupied the gaddí, or between the years, A.D. 1827 and 1845.

The whole of the inscription may be seen on Plate III. fig. 4, which is taken from a wax impression of the die from which the coins were struck, the size of an average coin is shown at fig. 7 of the same plate. On the obverse *Bádsháh 'Álam* can be read.

Weight. About 271 grains.

PARTÁBGARH CURRENCIES

PARTÁBGARH

CAPITAL PARTÁBGARH

The area of Partábgarh (Pratápgarh) is 959 square miles; it had, in 1891, a population of 87,975, or 91 persons per square mile. The revenue of the State is about £60,000 a year.

The State was founded by Surajmal, uncle to the celebrated Ráná Sangrám of Mewár, in the time of Ráná Raimal who reigned over Mewár from A.D. 1474 to 1509.

THE MINT

The mint located at the capital was opened in A.D. 1784. No gold coins have ever been struck, but silver and copper have been issued to very considerable amounts.

The silver coins are known by the name of Sálim Sháhí,[1] they were first issued by Sálim Siṇha, a former Chief, in the year 1784. The mint has been worked irregularly; from 1867 to 1869 no silver coins were made. In 1870 the Maháráwul reported to Col. J. P. Nixon, the Resident in Mewár, that copper had not been coined for a long time past (from Col. Nixon's letter to the Agent to the Governor-General for Rájputána, dated Feb. 25th, 1870).

The silver coins of the State are not only current in the Partábgarh territory, but also in Dúngárpur, in Bánswára, and throughout a large part of Málwah. It is said that the Sálim Sháhí coins were at one time also minted at Bánswára, and on some of the specimens inspected I have read *Zarab Báns—zarab Bánswára*?

The silver coins, as will be seen from the the following table, have been of very varied worth.

Old mint-marks given by Prinsep, *Useful Tables*, Pl. xlvi.

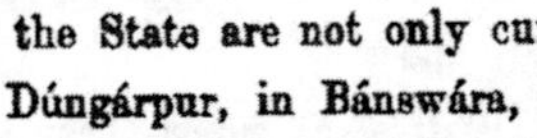

[1] The term *Shahi* attached to the designation of a coin refers to the monarch's "reign." The word *Sahi* signifies "impress" or "stamp."

SÁLIM SHÁHÍ RUPEES

Names.	Weight.	Value of 100 in Imperial Coin.	Pure contents.
Oldest or "Jurmuría."	168.50.	90.909.	150 grains.
"Murmuría," coined A.D. 1810.	168.50.	87.878.	145 grains.
"Meláh," coined A.D. 1820.	168.50.	83.030.	137 grains.
Rupee of "sanah 29."	168.11.	78.748.	......
Rupee of "sanah 45."	168.55.	82.148.	......
New Sálim Sháhí.	168.50.	....	......

Mr. A. Macdonald, reporting on the coinage of this State on the 13th of August, 1823, says: "The Rájá engaged in 1821 to reform his coinage, but it has never been done." As will be seen from the above table, the quantity of alloy had been increased from 18.5 grains to 31.5 grains in the rupee. On the 10th of September, 1824 the Government of the East India Company issued an order to the Rájá for the reform of the coinage, and, as the order was not attended to, it was enforced in the December of 1826. The issue of the coin bearing *sanah* 29, must have been of short duration, limited to the interval between the coining of the last "Meláh rupees" and the year 1823, for in the latter year the coin bearing *sanah* 45 was introduced. The *sanah* 45 rupees were issued to our troops at the exchange rate of 122.8 per 130 Farukhábád rupees.

Prinsep says[1] that the Partábgarh rupees bear a triple bow or knot, and an inscription in Nágarí character, and that the Sálim Sháhí rupee has a jháṛ or six-leaved branch. These statements I believe to be incorrect. The rupee with the Nágarí character and the triple bow is no doubt the Bajrangarh coin, see Plate VIII. figs. 17; I have never met with a Sálim Sháhí coin bearing a jháṛ, and I believe I have seen coins of all ages. The Bajrangarh Rupee, which is coined by a petty Zamíndár, is fully described in Prinsep's work.[2] The Bajrangarh estate is under the Central Indian Agency.

[1] *Useful Tables*, p. 64.   [2] *Op. cit.* pp. 64-65.

SILVER COINAGE

There have been two distinct issues as far as inscription is concerned, the old coins and the new Sálim Sháhí.

1. The old Sálim Sháhí. The pieces were the rupee and eight-anna bit. See Plate III., fig. 9.

INSCRIPTION. (In Persian letters of peculiar form.)

Obverse. سکه مبارک بادشاه غازي شاه عالم ۱۱۹۹ (۱۲۳۶)

Sikka mubárak bádsháh ghází Sháh 'Álam, 1199 (or 1236).

"Auspicious coin of the victorious Emperor Sháh 'Álam, A.H. 1199."

Reverse. ضرب . . . . سنة ۲۵ جلوس میمنت مانوس

Zarab . . . . *sanah* 25 (29 *or* 45) *julús maimanat mánus.*

"Struck in the 25th year of his fortunate reign."

The dates 1199 and 1236 are the Hijrí years corresponding to A.D. 1784 and 1820 respectively. Many different dies were used for these rupees during the long period in which they were issued, and, as is to be expected, the specimens exhibit slight differences, these, however, are very unimportant. On the edges of these coins different marks are to be seen, viz., a cross, a star, a circle with a dot in the centre, a crescent, and a mark like an English capital "L." (Similar marks are to be found on the Udaipurí and Chittorí coins of Mewár.)

The coins are easily distinguished by the peculiar conformation of the Persian letters, which are unlike those on any other coins in Rájputána.

The original rate of the rupee was fixed at 127.12 Sálim Sháhí coins to be equivalent to 100 Company rupees.

2. The new Sálim Sháhí coins. These were probably introduced about the year 1870, the pieces are the rupee, eight-anna, four-anna, and two-anna bits. See Plate III. fig. 18, and for the sizes of the smaller coins figs. 10, 11, and 12.

INSCRIPTION.

Obverse. سکه مبارک شاه لندن ۱۲۳۶ بادشاه غازي

Sikka mubárak Sháh London, 1236, *bádsháh ghází.*

"Auspicious coin of the noble monarch, the sovereign of London, A.H. 1236." (The old date 1236, A.D. 1820, being retained from the former die.)

Reverse. ضرب . . . . . سنة ۴۵ جلوس میمنت مانوس

Zarab . . . . . *sanah* 45 *julús maimanat mánús.*

"Struck in the 45th year of his fortunate reign." (Retained from the old coin.)

The Persian letters are very much better formed on the coins from some dies than on those from others.

Value. Nearly 13 annas Imperial.

COPPER COINAGE

1. The old paisá can be seen depicted at Plate III. fig. 19. The portion printed in dots shows the completion of the design on the obverse.

Inscription. ।।'रता।।
।थासव ?
(स ?)असमव
१९३५ = 1935.

Weight. About 120 grains.

2. The new copper coin. See Plate III. fig. 20.

Inscription.

Obverse. A rude representation of the sun and of two swords, within a circle surrounded by a circle of dots.

Reverse. In Nagárí character, प्रतापगढ रयासत १९४३.

Partábgarh riyásat 1943 (Pratápgarh). The date within an oval.

"Partábgarh State 1943" (A.D. 1886).

Weight. 120 grains.

DÚNGÁRPUR CURRENCIES

DÚNGÁRPUR

CAPITAL DÚNGÁRPUR

The Dúngárpur Chief is of the Udaipur family. In the 12th century Rahup, the eldest son of the Ráná, abandoned his claim to the throne of Chitor to his younger brother Mahup, and settled at Dúngárpur, which his descendant now holds together with the surname of "Ahária," signifying at which period in the history of the family his ancestor branched off from the stem. The title of the Dúngárpur Chief is "Ráwul" or "Maháráwul."

Dúngárpur, which is so called from the word "Dúngra," a mountain, has an area of 1440 square miles, with a population in 1891 of 165,400, or 115 persons per square mile. The revenue of the State is about £18,000 a year.

THE COINAGE

The Maháráwul states that his ancestors enjoyed the right of coining from time immemorial. In a kharíta to Colonel Nixon, formerly Resident in Mewár, dated Dec. 8th, 1868, the Chief stated that "sixty years previously there had been a mint at his capital where the 'old Chitore,' the 'Tursoolea,' and the 'Putreeserea' rupees were coined, but that owing to the unsettled state of the country the mint was closed." In 1887, I instituted an enquiry as to the correctness of this statement, my friend the Maháráwul assured me that no such coins as the "Tursoolea" and "Putreeserea" rupees had ever been made in the State, and I have been unable to find any specimens of coins with such names. It is likely enough that the "Old Chitor" rupees were also minted at Dúngárpur.

The only coin which can now be recognized as having been made in the State, is the "Dúngárpur Paisá." See Plate III. fig. 8. This coin was issued from the mint during the years 1860 and 1861. It bears on the obverse in Nágarí character, the words *Sirká Girpur*, meaning "The Government, the Hill City." On the reverse is the date, Samvat 1917–18 (A.D. 1860–1), a sword, and a jháṛ.

सरकारगड़पर (for गिरपुर) १९१७ 

Weight. 160 grains.

BÁNSWÁRA CURRENCIES

BÁNSWÁRA

CAPITAL BÁNSWÁRA

The area of Bánswára is 1505 square miles. The population in 1891 was 180,915, or 120 persons per square mile. The revenue is supposed to be about £28,000 a year.

The Bánswára House is a junior branch of the Dúngárpur family. On the death of Udaya Siṇha in 1528, the kingdom of Dúngárpur was divided between his two sons, the Mahi river being fixed on as the boundary between the two States. Towards the end of the 18th century, Bánswára became more or less subject to the Maráthás; and it paid tribute to the Chief of Dhar in Central India. In 1818 the treaty with the British Government was concluded.

The title of the Chief is "Mahárávul."

THE MINT

Only one mint has been worked in this State. No Jágírdárs have ever coined money. When, on Feb. 25th, 1870, Colonel J. P. Nixon wrote to the Agent to the Governor-General on the subject of the Bánswára mint, he reported that the Chief claimed the right of coining. At that time only copper was being minted; shortly after the correspondence the Government issued orders that no new coins were to be introduced into circulation from any of the mints of the Native Princes. In spite of this order, and indeed shortly after it was received, the Bánswára Chief issued the Lachman Sháhí silver pieces, which he still continues to coin.

SILVER COINAGE

The Lachman Sháhí coins, which were issued by the present Chief soon after the year 1870. See Plate III. fig. 13, which is taken from a wax cast of the die at the Bánswára mint. Figs. 14, 15, and 16 show average sizes of the rupee, eight-anna, and four-anna pieces. Both surfaces of the coins show the same inscription, which is unintelligible even to the Durbár officials.

Weight of the Rupee 123 grains, and of the smaller pieces in proportion.

Value of the rupee 13 annas Imperial.

It is stated that in former days the Sálim Sháhí rupee (see Partábgarh) was coined at Bánswára, it certainly was the rupee of the State and still has a large circulation in the Maháráwul's territory.

COPPER COINAGE

Lachman Sháhí paisá. In a Kharíta from the Maháráwul to the Resident in Mewár, dated 30th June, 1869, it is stated that the copper coins then being made at the mint were 7 máshas in weight, and were sold at the rate of 80 for a Sálim Sháhí or Udaipur rupee, the value in Imperial money being $\frac{2}{25}$ of a British anna.

The coin now known as the Lachman Sháhí paisá is depicted on Plate III. fig. 17. I have not been able to obtain any details about this coin, but it is not the one spoken of in the above-mentioned kharíta.

Weight. 120 grains.

MÁRWÁR CURRENCIES

JODHPUR

AND OTHER TYPES.

PLATE IV

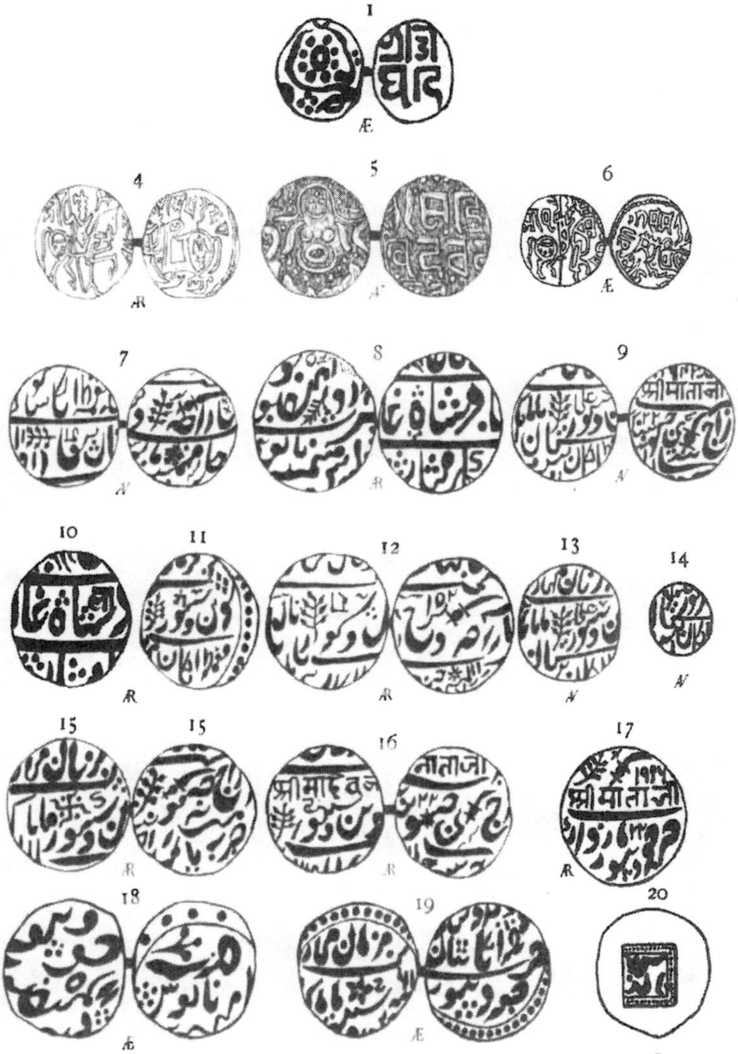

KÚCHÁWAN

MÁRWÁR

CAPITAL JODHPUR

Márwár is a corruption of Maru-varsha (Marvád), "the desert region," a name which anciently comprehended the entire desert from the Sutlej to the ocean, but which is now restricted to the country subject to the main branch of the Ráhtor race. The area of this country is 37,445 square miles; in the early part of this century the population was estimated at two millions, but by the 1891 census it numbered 2,521,727, or 67 persons per square mile; the revenue is about £400,000 a year.

Legend states that the first Ráhtor sprung from the spine of Indra, the father of the race being Yavanaswa, a prince of Scythic origin from beyond the Indus—a Yavan of the Aswa tribe, the latter being one of the four tribes which overturned the Greek kingdom of Bactria.

In Samvat 526 (A.D. 470), Nayana Pála, a lineal descendant from Yavanaswa, conquered Kanauj and founded the great Ráhtor kingdom on the shores of the Ganges, and hence the family derived the appellation of "Kanaujea Ráhtor."

In the days of its glory, Kanauj is said to have had a circumvallation covering a space of more than thirty miles. The army of its Rájá, Jaya Siṇha, to oppose the Yavana, beyond the Indus, is said to have consisted of 80,000 men in armour, of 30,000 horses covered with quilted mail, of 300,000 infantry, of 200,000 men with bows and battle-axes, and of a cloud of elephants bearing warriors.

The Ráhtor kingdom of Kanauj extended northwards to the foot of the snowy mountains, eastward to Benares and across the Chumbul to the lands of Bandelkhand, while on the south its territory bordered on Mewár. In the days of Jaya Siṇha's zenith, the lord of the Chohans and the Ráná of Mewár are said to have been the only princes of India who denied his supremacy.

In A.D. 1194, Sháhábuddín, king of Ghor, after overthrowing the Chohan prince Prithiráj, turned his arms against the Ráhtoras of Kanauj. Jaychand, the Rájá, was conquered, the mighty kingdom was wrecked, her capital and army destroyed, and from that time Kanauj ceased to be a Hindú city, and the name of Ráhtor vanished from the banks of the Ganges. Eighteen years later, Seoji (Siraji) and Saitrám, grandsons of Jaychand, abandoning the land of their birth, with 200 retainers journeyed westward to settle in the "desert region." In eleven generations the race had so multiplied that the chief was able to assault Mundore, to slay the prince of the ancient Purihar race, and to plant the "pancharanga" (five-coloured banner) of Kanauj on the walls of the ancient capital of Maru. The conquests of Nagore and of Nadole, the capital of the province of Godwar, soon followed. In less than four centuries, the descendants of the exiles occupied the whole desert; they had founded three capitals, studded the land with their feudal castles, and were able to bring into the field 50,000 men, "sons of one father," to resist the Muhammadan power.

In Samvat, 1484, the celebrated Jodha was born, and in S. 1515 (A.D. 1459) he laid the foundations of Jodhpur, whither he transferred the seat of his Government from Mundore.

Jodhpur is situated on Yodhagiri ("the hill of warriors"), an elevation of the same range as that on which Mundore stands, and distant from the latter named place about four miles in a southerly direction. In speaking of Jodgir (Yodhagiri), Tod says "its scarped summit renders it almost impregnable, while its superior elevation permits the sons of Joda to command, from the windows of their palace, a range of vision almost comprehending the limits of their sway. In clear weather they can view the summits of their southern barrier, the gigantic Aravalli; but in every other direction it fades away in the boundless expanse of sandy plains."

The great Akbar invaded Márwár in A.D. 1561, and granted to the then ruling chief, Maldeo, the title of "Rájá Rájeswár," or "Rájá, lord of Rájás." A few years later Maldeo succumbed to necessity, sent his sons with gifts to the Emperor at Ajmere (the elder was enrolled among the "commanders of a thousand"), and became a vassal of the empire. Under Maldeo's successor, Udaya Sinha, the union of the Imperial-house with that of Jodhpur took place, by the marriage of Jodh Bai to Akbar. On that occasion the Emperor restored all the possessions which he had wrested from his bride's house, with the exception of Ajmere.

From S. 1786 (A.D. 1729) the political independence of Márwár dates, for then the real dismemberment of the Empire began.

In S. 1809 (A.D. 1753) Bijy Siṇha succeeded to the gaddí. His long reign (S. 1809 to S. 1850) was disturbed by intestine troubles and by the inroads of the Maráthás, who had obtained a footing in Rájwárra. From this time Márwár knew no continued peace until the treaty with the East India Company was concluded. In S. 1874, or December, A.D. 1817, the treaty was negociated at Dehlí by a Brahmın named Byás Bishen Rám, on the part of the Prince-Regent; and in December, A.D. 1818, Mr. Wilder, the political superintendent of Ajmere, was deputed to report on the condition of the country.

LIST OF THE MAHARAJAS FROM A.D. 1751 TO THE PRESENT DAY

Name	Date of ascending the Gaddi	Date of death
1. Mahárájá Bakhat Siṇha.	A.D. 1751.	A.D. 1752.
2. Mahárájá Bijy Siṇha (Vijaya Siṇha).	A.D. 1752.	A.D. 1792.
3. Mahárájá Bhím Siṇha.	A.D. 1792.	A.D. 1803.
4. Mahárájá Mán Siṇha.	A.D. 1803.	A.D. 1843.
5. Mahárájá Takhat Siṇha.	A.D. 1843.	A.D. 1873.
6. H.H. Mahárájá Jaswant Siṇha, G.C.S.I.	A.D. 1873.	Now reigning.

A list of the earlier Chiefs is given in Prinsep's *Useful Tables*, pp. 258-259.

When the Ráhtors settled in the desert, they doubtless carried with them such part of the coined treasure of Kanauj as their conquerors had allowed them to retain, and it is not unlikely that the exiled Chiefs and their successors continued for some time to coin money from dies similar to those used in the latter days of their ancient kingdom. Coins of the Kanauj types (of Jaychand and other Rájás) are frequently found in Rájputána, and copper specimens are still in circulation in the Bázárs. See Plate IV. figs. 1 and 5 (these coins are found in considerable abundance).

Obverse. A rudely executed front view of a female seated in the native fashion, a glory round the head, and holding the cornucopia.

Reverse. In a more modern style of Nágarí :—*S'rímad Govinda Chandra-deva*, *S'rí Ajaya deva*, or *S'rímad Jadjeya deva*, or kindred inscriptions.

From the time of the establishment of their power in the desert until the decline of the Muhammadan power, the Ráhtors seldom knew the sweets of peace and independence, and it is unlikely that they coined money on their own account to any extent. For a long period they were subject to the Dehlí Emperors who denied to their vassals the exercise of the ancient right of coining money. I believe I am correct in stating that, between the issues of the more modern of the Kanauj coins and those struck during the decline of the Empire, no coins were struck by the Ráhtors, or, at all events, none now exist, which can be with certainty attributed to the Ráhtor princes; nor do, as far as I have been able to discover, any records of mints or coins of the Jodhpur State exist save those mentioned hereafter. It is probable that, during this long period, the coins of the Muhammadan invaders were those chiefly used in Rájwárra—they were certainly the current coins in Márwár from the days of the invasion of Akbar, until the State again asserted her independence.

The earliest Márwár coins, of which I have found mention, are those of Ajít. I have not been able to procure specimens, and know not in what metal the coins were made. Tod, in his Rájast'hán, mentions that, in S. 1777 (A.D. 1720), Ajít coined money in his own name. In S. 1766 (A.D. 1709) he had received the sunnud of the nine castles of Maru from the Emperor Aurungzeb. He entered Jodhpur in Sáwan 1767, and in the same year helped to place Muhammad Sháh on the throne of Dehlí; he drove the Muslím from Ajmere.

The Jodhpur coinage in its present form was commenced during the decline of the Muhammadan power in India. Bijy (Beejy) Siṇha began the issue, he struck coins in the days of and name of Sháh 'Álam (A.D. 1759—1786). Before the days of the Bijy Sháhí coins those of the Muhammadan Dehlí Emperors were current in Márwár.

Mahárájá Bijy Siṇha reigned over Márwár from A.D. 1752 to 1792. He is said to have opened his mint in A.D. 1761. The name of "Bíjy Sháhí" has been continued to the present day; and until the year A.D. 1858 the name and symbols of Sháh 'Álam were continued on the coins issued. In 1858 the Queen's name was substituted for that of the Dehlí Emperor at the Jodhpur-town mint, but the introduction of the dies bearing reference to the British supremacy was later at some

JODHPUR

PLATE V

(From wax casts of the dies)

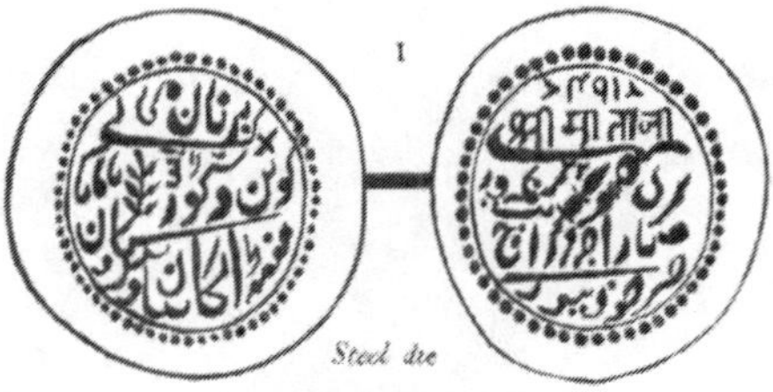

Steel die

JODHPUR TOWN

2

Steel die

6

AR

5

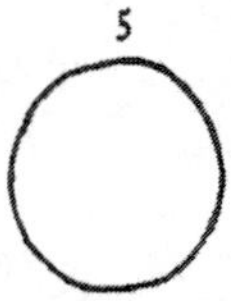

AR

SUJAT

7

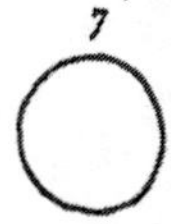

AR

3

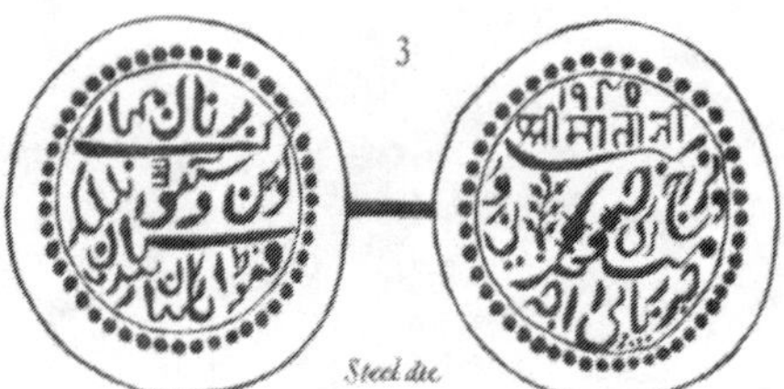

Steel die

PALÍ

4

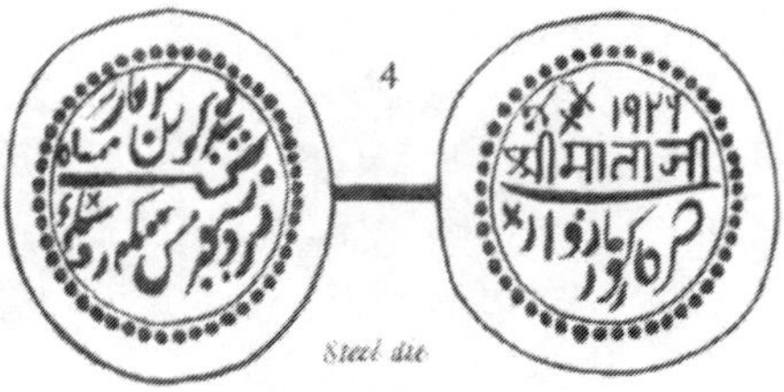

Steel die

NAGORE

of the provincial mints, for the Lullúlía rupees coined at Sújat in 1859 still bore the name of the Muhammadan Emperor.

The coins of the State are of gold, silver, and copper, and are current over the whole of Márwár.

No "nazr" coins have ever been struck in the State.

MINTS

Mints have been located at the following places in the State—at Jodhpur (the capital town), at Nagore, at Palí, and at Sújat. No coins have been issued from the Sújat and Nagore mints since Samvats 1945 (A.D. 1888) and 1929 (A.D. 1872) respectively. The Jodhpur and Palí mints are still regularly worked. New dies are introduced at each of the mints for silver coins, and at the Jodhpur-town mint for gold, on the 18th of Sáwan Budh in each year, this being the day when the new Samvat begins. Since Samvat 1918 (A.D. 1863) coins have been struck by the Durbár bearing the Samvat year in which they were issued.

The dies for the copper coins are not changed yearly, but only when it is necessary.

The coins from the different mints can be distinguished by the formation and arrangement of the letters in the inscriptions, and by the following characteristics:—In the coins from the Jodhpur-town mint the special mark of the mint dároga is adjacent to the jhár on the obverse side, and as a rule the coins bear the name "Srí Mátají." In the Palí coins the mint dároga's special mark is on the side other than that bearing the jhár, that is to say it is on the obverse, the jhár being on the reverse side near to the sword. The specimens from the Nagore mint do not bear a sword below the Hindí letters on the reverse. A part of, or an entire jhár, and a part of, or an entire sword are figured above the Hindí letters on the reverse. Some of the Sújat coins bear a katári or dagger. The mint dároga's mark is near to the jhár on the obverse. Some of the coins bear the name "Srí Mahá Deva."

It is the custom of the country that each newly-appointed "Dároga" (mint-master) of the "Taksál" (mint) chooses some special mark or device of his own, whereby the coins issued by him, and for which he is responsible, may be easily recognized, hence the large number of small marks and devices found on the coins of the State.

The following are examples of marks placed on the coins by dárogas, or by other State officials:—

1.  Mark found on the coin issued by Kani Rám, dároga of the Jodhpur-town mint from S. 1906 (A.D. 1849) to S. 1919 (A.D. 1862). ग (G), the first letter of "Gungsharám," a deity much worshipped at Jodhpur, and to whom the ancient Ráj Mandir at that place is dedicated.

2.  Mark found on the "Rururía rupees" coined in S. 1923 (A.D. 1866) by Anar Siṇha, dároga of the Jodhpur-town mint, being the first letters of "Ravana ra sath," or of "Radha." (See Rururía rupee.)

3. علی Mark of dároga Mumtaz Ali, who held the post at the Jodhpur-town mint from A.D. 1884 to 1886.

4. ट Mark of Bohra Gokal Chand, dároga of the Sújat mint from Chait Budh VII., Samvat 1936 (A.D. 1878) to Kátik Budh III., Samvat 1938 (A.D. 1881). See Plate IV. fig. 16.

5. का Mark of Bias Kishen Das, dároga of the Sújat mint when the last coins were made there in Samvat 1945 (A.D. 1888).

6.  Swastika emblem, used by Joshi Hans Ráj on the coins made at Palí in the time of Mahárájá Takhat Siṇha. (See Plate IV. fig. 15.)

7. मृा Mark introduced into the coins made at Palí by Lala Sedh Mal, hákim or governor of that Province. It is an abbreviation of "Máhá Deva."

8. बा Mark introduced by Mangal Chand, who succeeded Sedh Mal as hákim of Palí in A.D. 1886. It forms the first syllable of "Bálájí," whose devout worshipper he was.

The "jháṛ" and the "sword" are the special marks of the Márwár or Jodhpur State. The jháṛ is one of seven or nine branches. The nine-branched jháṛ is found on the original Bijy Sháhí rupee and on the Lullulía coins. Its local name is "Turra," signifying an ornament worn on the turban; this name is said to have been introduced by Mahárájá Takhat Siṇha. The local name of the "sword" mark is "khanda."

The marks displayed in the margin, which are found on some of the coins of the State, are said by the officials to be without significance, merely being added to fill up spaces and to give the coins an ornamental appearance. On a large number of the old coins of the State, and indeed on some of the coins bearing the Queen's name (blindly copied by some ignorant artificer from an old coin, without reference to meaning), the Persian numerals ۲۲ (22) are found. The number refers to the 22nd year of the reign of Sháh 'Álam, A.D. 1781, which was probably the year in which the Emperor gave his consent to the issue of the Bijy Sháhí rupee, though, as before related, they were first struck twenty years earlier, in the year A.D. 1761.

GOLD COINAGE

At the present time gold is only coined at the Jodhpur-town mint, and it is said that gold has never been issued from the provincial mints.

The gold coins of the State are the muhr, half-muhr, and quarter-muhr. They are known as the Jodhpur Muhr, etc. The gold coins of the State are uncommon, and are rarely met with beyond the Márwár borders.

1. The muhr bearing Sháh 'Álam's name has the same inscription as the Bijy Sháhí silver coins of A.D. 1761 (see Plate IV. fig. 8, and silver coins No 1, p. 44). Gold was probably first coined in A.D. 1781, and from the same die as that from which the silver pieces were struck. These coins were issued up to and during the early part of the reign of Mahárájá Takhat Siṇha, who came into his early inheritance in 1843.

2. Takhat Siṇha's first muhr (see Plate IV. fig. 7).

INSCRIPTION.

Obverse. کوین وکٹوریہ ملکہ معظمہ انگلستان و ہندوستان ضرب
دار الم نصور جودہپور

Queen Victoria malika mu'azzamah Inglistán wa Hindústán Zarab-i-dár-al manṣúr Jodhpur.

"G" for "Gungsharam." A "jháṛ" placed horizontally over "dár-al."

"Her Majesty Queen Victoria of England and India. Struck in the house of victory, Jodhpur."

Reverse. سنة جلوس ميمنت مانوس مهاراج‌ادراج سري تخت سنگه بهادر

Sanah julús maimanat mánús Mahárájádhiráj S'ri Takhat Singh Bahádar.

"In the year of the fortunate reign of Mahárájádhirája Takhat Singh."

Symbols. The jháṛ and the sword.

I should have thought from its style and make, that this coin was issued from the Palí mint. However, I am assured that gold was never coined there.

3. Takhat Siṇha's muhr of 1869 and the following years. This coin is struck from a die exactly similar to that used in the stamping of the silver coins of the same date (see Plate IV. fig. 17, and Plate V. fig. 4).

4. The gold coins of H.H. Jaswant Siṇha (1873 to the present day). They bear the same inscription as the silver coins of the same dates (see Plate IV. figs. 9, 13, and 14. The first shows the muhr. Nos. 13 and 14 show the sizes of the ¼ and ½ muhr respectively). The arrangement of the inscription is, however, slightly different to that found on the silver coins, the Persian character is also more distinctly stamped.

Weight. The muhrs, old and new, weigh 169.9 grains Troy, and the smaller pieces are in exact proportion.

Assay. The coins are of pure gold.

SILVER COINAGE

The silver coins of the State are the rupee, half-rupee, and quarter-rupee pieces.

1. Original Bijy Sháhí coins (see Plate IV. fig. 8, but in silver), A D 1761-1858.

Obverse. سکه مبارک بادشاه غازي شاه عالم

Sikka mubárak bádsháh ghází Sháh 'Álam.

"Auspicious coin of the noble monarch Sháh 'Álam."

Reverse. جلوس میمنت مانوس ضرب دار الم نصور جودپور
Julús maimanat mánús zarab-i-dár-al mansúr Jodhpur.

"Struck in the house of victory Jodhpur in the year of his fortunate reign."

Weight. The weight is said by the Jodhpur officials to be 176.4 grains. The Calcutta assay tables make the coins a little more.

Assay. Said to be 9 máshas 6 rattis of silver, and 3 rattis of alloy, or silver 169.9 grains and alloy 6.5 grains Troy in the rupee. The alloy is therefore about ۱/۲۷ part.

2. The coins issued in 1858 (the first to bear the Queen's name) and those issued in 1863 (see Plate IV. fig. 12, but minus the LL on the reverse).

INSCRIPTION.

Obverse. بزمان مبارک کوین وکٹوریه ملکه معظمه انگلستان و هندوستان
Bazamán-i-mubárak Queen Victoria malikah mu'azzamah Inglistán wa Hindústán.

"During the auspicious reign of her Majesty Queen Victoria of England and India."

Reverse. مهاراجادراج سري تخت سنگه بهادر ضرب جودپور
Mahárájádhiráj Sri Takhat Singh bahádur zarab-i-Jodhpur.

"Struck at Jodhpur by Mahárájádhirája Takhat Singh."

3. About the year A.D. 1859, in the reign of Mahárájá Takhat Siṇha, the eunuch, Nazar Harkaran, was appointed to the charge of the Sújat mint. He coined about a lakh of rupees with a proportion of alloy of one part in twenty-five instead of one part in twenty-seven, and he stamped the letters ला (LA') on the obverse over the word "Sháh." The letters are the first two of "Láll Bábá," the name of his "Ish Dev" or tutelar divinity. These rupees are known by the name of Lullulía ("Lulluleea" or "Lullulasahi"). They are avoided by the traders.

INSCRIPTION.

The same as on the rupees coined from 1761 to 1858.

Weight. The weight is 175 grains. (See Plate IV. fig. 10.)

4. Gungsharám Rupee (see Plate IV. fig. 11). These coins were struck at the Jodhpur-town mint by Kaní Rám, some time before the year A.D. 1862, they bear the same inscription as the coins of 1858 with a "ग" (G). (See mint marks, No. 1, p. 42.)

Weight. The weight of the rupee is 176 grains.

5. Rururía Rupee. In A.D. 1866 (S. 1923), Anar Siṇha, alias Aují, the brother of Mahárájá Takhat Siṇha's favourite slave girl, was appointed dároga of the Jodhpur-town mint. He also issued coins with a larger amount of alloy than the Bijy Sháhí rupees should contain. He stamped the letters "रा" (RÁ) on his coins, which are known by the name of "Rururías." These rupees are refused by the merchants. To account for the "रा" on the issue, it is said by some that the letters are the first two of "Rádhá," the name of one of the frail beauties of the town; by others it is stated that the letters are the first two of *Rávana rá Sath*, a Márwár courtesy title given to Aují, he being a "gola" or "slave" by caste.

INSCRIPTION.

The same inscription as on the coins issued in 1858, but with the special mark as before noted (see Plate IV. fig. 12).

6. In 1869 the inscription was altered on the dies. The coins of 1869, 1870, and a few succeeding years bear the following inscription :—

Obverse. بعهد کوین شاه هند و فرنگ زرو سیم را سکه زد تخت سنگه

Ba-áhdi Queen Sháh-i Hindo Farung zaro sím rá sikka zad Takhat Singh.

"By permission of her Majesty the Queen of India and England Takhat Singh struck gold and silver coins."

Reverse. श्री माताजी ۱۹۲۶ ضرب جودپور ماروار

Sri Mátáji (in Hindi). *Zarab-i Jodhpur Márwár* 1926 (in Persian character). The date 1869 or 1870. The jháṛ and sword in entirety or part.

"Struck at Jodhpur, Márwár."

See Plate V. fig. 4 (a Nagore coin on which the inscription is very imperfect), and Plate IV. fig. 17 (but in silver), a coin of S. 1926, or A.D. 1869, probably from the mint at the capital. It bears the Persian numerals ۲۲ (22), for the explanation of which circumstance see page 43.

Weight. The weight of this rupee is 176 grains.

7. Between the years 1878 and 1881 A.D., coins were issued from the Sújat mint, by dároga Bohra Gokal Chand, with *Srí Mátájí* on the reverse, and *Srí Máhádevjí* (for Máhádevají) on the obverse, in Hindí letters. (See Plate IV. fig. 16.) The rest of the inscription on these coins is the same as that on the specimens struck at Sújat of late years. The full inscription and its arrangement may be seen at Plate V. fig. 2.

8. Silver coins of Jaswant Siṇha (1873 to date). See Plate V. figs. 1, 2, and 3.

INSCRIPTION:

Obverse. بزمان مبارک کوین وکٹوریه ملکه معظمه انگلستان و هندوستان
Bazamán-i mubárak Queen Victoria malikah mu'azzamah Inglistán wa Hindústán.

"During the auspicious reign of Her Majesty Queen Victoria of England and India."

Reverse. श्री माताजी ۱۹۴۱ مهاراج ادراج سري جسونت سنگه
بهادر ضرب جودپور

Mahárájádhirája S'rí Jaswant Siṇha bahádur zarab-i-Jodhpur. And the Samvat in Persian character. In Hindí the words *S'rí Mátájí.*

"Struck at Jodhpur by Mahárájá Jaswant Siṇha, 1941." "S'rí Mátájí."

(Plate V. figs. 5, 6, and 7, show the sizes of the rupee, eight-anna, and four-anna pieces respectively.)

COPPER COINAGE

The original copper coin of the State was the Bijy Sháhí, which was also called "Dhabú Sáhí" on account of its great weight. In the time of Bhím Singh, A.D. 1792–1803, the name was changed to "Bhím Sháhí," and the weight of the coins was increased by two máshas. The Bhím Sháhí coin is still used as the standard in the weighing of opium, its value in Imperial money is nearly six pies. The weight of the copper coin was afterwards reduced to the first standard. The copper coins are now generally known by the name "Dhabú Sáhí." The copper money is not made at the State mints, but by certain traders, who pay a royalty of three rupees per maund for the privilege of coining it. The Dhabú coins are also current in the Sirohi State which is ruled over by the Deora Prince (Chohan).

1. Bhím or Bijy Sháhí (see Plate IV. fig. 18).

INSCRIPTION.

Obverse. سنه جلوس میمنت مانوس ضرب

Sanah julús maimanat mánús zarab.

"Struck in the year of his fortunate reign."

Symbols. A jháṛ of three points, or a dároga's mark—

Reverse. دار المنصور جودپور

Dar-ul mansúr Jodhpur.

"In the house of victory, Jodhpur."

Weight. The weight is from 310 to 320 grains.

2. The new copper coin (see Plate IV. fig. 19).

INSCRIPTION.

Obverse. بزمان مبارک کوین وکتوریه ملکه سنه

Bazamán-i-mubárak Queen Victoria malikah, sanah.

Mint-mark.

Reverse. معظمه انگلستان و هندوستان ضرب جودپور

Mu'azzamah Inglistán wa Hindústán zarab Jodhpur.

"Struck at Jodhpur in the .... year of the auspicious reign of Her Majesty Queen Victoria of England and India."

Weight. From 310 to 320 grains.

3. The Amir Sháhí coin (see Plate IV. fig. 20). This piece was introduced by Amir Siṇha, elder brother to the Mahárájá Jaswant Siṇha, to whom the Emperor Sháh Jahán (A.D. 1628 to 1658) had given the pargana of Nagore in jágir. The coins must have been issued over a considerable period, but the coining of them has been long discontinued. The coins are without impress on one surface, on the other they bear

an inscription in Persian characters within a square border (see the drawing).

Weight. The coins average 255 grains in weight.

TABLE SHOWING THE QUANTITIES OF GOLD, SILVER, AND COPPER COINED IN THE JODHPUR STATE FROM THE YEAR 1884 TO THE END OF 1891

Year	Gold Coins	Silver Coins	Copper Coins
1884—1885	18,753	99,196	425,802
1885—1886	12,831	233,369	4,886
1886—1887	Has not	yet been ascer	tained.
1887—1888	13,363	385,052	11,147
1888—1889	18,005	350,663	418,725
1889—1890	26,403	505,131	No return.
1890—1891	28,183	82,919	16,714

Old mint-marks of the State according to Prinsep,[1] but unknown to me:—

Jodhpur— 

Palí— 

Nagore— 

KUCHAWAN

The only vassal of the Jodhpur Ráj allowed to coin is the Takhur of Kuchawan. The Takhur belongs to the clan Udawut, and in the Durbár he ranks as the first noble in the second class; his revenue is said to be about 50,000 rupees a year, an amount considerably greater than the revenue of many of the first-class nobles. Kuchawan is a "bhúm" or allodial estate, internally independent except in very important cases. Kuchawan, the capital town of the country, is a walled city situated on an elevation of considerable height. From the fortress an extensive view is obtained of the surrounding country; it is situated on the sand-track or road leading from the railway station at Phalera to Bíkaner.

[1] *Useful Tables*, pl. xlvi.

LIST OF THE KUCHAWAN TAKHURS A.D. 1725 TO DATE

Name	Date of Succession	Date of Death
Takhur Zálim Singh	1725	....
Takhur Sabha Singh	....	1757
Takhur Súraj Mal	1757	1790
Takhur Sheonath Singh	1790	1827
Takhur Ranjit Singh	1827	1857
Takhur Kesrí Singh[1]	1857	Now living

COINAGE

No gold or copper coins have ever been struck by the Kuchawan Takhurs.

Silver coinage. There have been two distinct issues of silver coins. The pieces are the rupee, eight-anna, and four-anna bits.

1. The old Kuchawan coins. They are styled "31 Sanda" (sanah). In Prinsep's *Useful Tables*,[2] they are called *Bopusáhi*. They are also sometimes called the *Borsi rupees* (see Plate IV. fig. 21). It is supposed that they were first coined in A.D. 1788, the thirty-first year of the Takhurship of Súraj Mal. The coins were at first struck at Ajmere (during the last century, as at earlier dates, Ajmere was several times in the possession of the Ráhtors of Márwár), and afterwards, when the mint was removed to Kuchawan, no change was made in the inscription on the dies until the introduction of the new issue.

INSCRIPTION.

Obverse. سکه مبارک بادشاه غازي شاه عالم

Sikka mubárak bádsháh ghási Sháh 'Alam.

"Auspicious coin of the victorious Emperor Sháh 'Alam."

Symbols. A sword over the *h* of *Sháh*. 

The date in Persian numerals.

[1] A grand old man, a faithful supporter of the British rule. When the writer passed through Kuchawan for the first time, on his way to Bikaner, Takhur Kesrí Singh met him some miles from his capital and paid him every honour; he introduced to him descendants to the third generation; each of the representatives of the four generations bears a different Hindu name, each name signifying a tiger.

[2] Page 68

Reverse. سنة ٣١ جلوس میمنت مانوس ضرب دار الخیر اجمیر

Sanah 31 *julús maimanat mánús zarab-i-dár-al-khair Ajmere.*

Struck at Ajmere, the seat of happiness, in the 31st year of his fortunate reign.

Weight. 166 grains.

Value. Ten annas, three pies, Imperial.

2. The new Kuchawan coins. Introduced in 1863. (See Plate IV. fig. 22, and for the average sizes of the smaller pieces figs. 23 and 24.)

INSCRIPTION.

Obverse. کوین وکٹوریه ملکه معظمه انگلستان و هندوستان

Queen Victoria malikah-mu'azzamah Inglistán wa Hindústán.

"Her Majesty Queen Victoria of England and India."

Symbols. A "flower" over the word "Queen."

Reverse. ضرب کچاون علاق جودهپور سنة عیوي ۱۸۶۳

Zarab Kuchawan 'allakah Jodhpur sanah 'Iywy (for *Iswy*), 1863.

"Struck at Kuchawan, in the State of Jodhpur, in the year of Jesus, 1863."

Weight. The average weight is 168 grains for the rupee, and for the two smaller pieces an exact proportion.

Value. About 12 annas and 3 pies, Imperial.

Bópusahí = 

The mint-marks figured in the margin are given in Prinsep's *Useful Tables*,[1] as belonging to the coins of this State. I have been unable to find any coins, belonging to the State, with such marks, and believe Prinsep's information to have been incorrect.

Assay. The coins are composed of 75 per cent. of silver and 25 per cent. of alloy.

The coins are current in the Kuchawan territory, in Kishangarh, and in parts of Márwár. They are much used by the bankers, and by the Rájputs in paying largess to temples, or to the Bháts and Charuns on the occasion of their marriage ceremonies. As the rupee is of less

[1] Pl. xlvi.

value than the Bijy Sháhí coin, the amount of the gift is magnified by $\frac{1}{4}$th when speaking of the number of rupees presented or spent. It was for this reason that the recommendation for the continuation of a mint at Kuchawan was made, by the Local Authorities, the last time an attempt was made by Government to reduce the number of coins in circulation in Rájputána. Now that the sums to be spent on marriage festivities have been settled by the Chiefs under the direction of Colonel C. K. M. Walter, C.S.I., late Agent to the Governor-General, the chief reason for allowing this mint to remain working has ceased to exist.

BÍKANER CURRENCIES

BI'KANER

CAPITAL BI'KANER

Area, 23,090 square miles. Population (in 1891), 831,955, or 36 persons per square mile. Revenue, about £160,000 a year.

The State was founded by Bíka, the 6th son of Jodha of Márwár. The line of greatest breadth extends from Púgul to Rájgarh, and measures 180 miles; the length from north to south, between Bhutnair and Máhájin, is about 160 miles.

It was in S. 1515 (A.D. 1459), the year in which Jodha transferred the seat of his government from Mundur to Jodhpur, that Bíka, under the guidance of his uncle Kandul, led three hundred of the sons of Seojí to enlarge the boundaries of the Ráhtor dominions amidst the sands of Maru. He first conquered the Sanklas of Janglú, and then marrying the daughter of the Bháttí Chief of Púgul, fixed his head-quarters at Korumdesir, where he erected a castle, and from thence gradually augmented his territories. With such rapidity were States formed in those times that in a few years he was lord over two thousand six hundred and seventy villages, and by a title far stronger and more legitimate than that of conquest—by the spontaneous election of the Jit Cantons.

It was in the district of Bhagur that Bíka founded his capital in S. 1545 (A.D. 1489), thirty years after leaving Mundur. The spot selected for the city was the birthright of a Jit, who would only concede it for the purpose on the condition that his name should be linked in perpetuity with its surrender. Naira was the name of the proprietor, which Bíka added to his own, thus composing that of his future capital.

Ráj Singh, who succeeded to the throne in A.D. 1573, was the prince who bartered his freedom to become a satrap of Dehlí. He had married a sister of one of Akbar's wives, and this connection obtained for him, on his introduction at Court by the Rájá of Amber, the dignity of a leader of 4,000 horse.

LIST OF THE CHIEFS FROM A.D. 1746 TO DATE

Name	Date of Accession	Date of Death	Age at Death
Mahárájá Gaj Singh	1746	1787	64 years
,, Ráj Singh	1787	1787	....
,, Súrut Singh	1787	1828	63 ,,
,, Ratan Singh	1828	1851	61 ,,
,, Sirdar Singh	1851	1872	54 ,,
,, Dúnga Singh	1872	1887	33 ,,
,, Ganga Singh	1887	Now living	

THE MINT

There are no records to show that a mint existed in the State from the time of the foundation of the kingdom to the day when the prince became a vassal of the Muhammadan Empire, nor do any coins exist which can be attributed to the early Rájás as far as I have been able to ascertain. The coins of the Empire were long those current in the State, and at the time of the foundation of the present mint the Faruk Sháhí was the rupee of the country (the coin of the Emperor Farukshir, A.D. 1713-1719).

The mint was opened by Mahárájá Gaj Singh, who obtained a sanad from the Emperor 'Álamgir 2nd, A.D. 1754-1759 (Aziz-ud-din Muhammad), permitting him to coin. It is stated by the Bíkaner officials, that the privilege was granted in S. 1809 (A.D. 1753), though the authorizing sanad is not now traceable. I do not believe that any coins were struck until after the year 1759, the first year of Sháh 'Álam's reign. From the time of Gaj Singh until the year A.D. 1859 all the coins of the State were struck in the name of Sháh 'Álam, in that year the Queen's name was first cut on the die.

Each Chief has adopted a special device for his coins, and by these symbols the coins can be easily recognized. The marks are as follows:

1. 

2. 

3. 

4. 

5. 

6. 

1. For Gaj Singh a "pataká" (dhvaja) or "flag." (Standard of Siva.)
2. For Súrut Singh a "trisúl" or "trident."
3. For Ratan Singh a "kirnia" or "turban-star."
4. For Sirdar Singh a "chhátá" or "umbrella."
5. For Dúnga Singh a "chaurí" or "fly-whisk."
6. For Ganga Singh a "morchhal" or "peacock-feather fly-whisk."

No gold coins have have ever been struck in the State, but each of the princes has issued silver and copper. The mint has always been located in the capital town.

The silver coins are well struck and are among the best in Rájputána. Both nazr and ordinary rupees were issued; the nazr coins are especially fine, and are generally of full weight. Before the time of Sirdar Singh no smaller silver coin than the rupee was issued. Sirdar and Dúnga Singh coined pieces of the value of a half, a quarter, and an eighth of a rupee. During the present reign no pieces of the value of an eighth of a rupee were coined until the year 1890.

In Prinsep's *Useful Tables*,[1] the weight of the Bíkaner rupee is given at 174 grains, and the pure contents is stated at 167.47 grains. The assay is stated as "Br. II," and the touch at 96 2. The value of 100 rupees is said to be 101.5 Imperial coins.

The full weight of the rupee ought to be 178 grains. I have never seen a well-stamped coin of less weight than 174 grains; they as a rule vary from 175 to 177 grains.

The value of 100 rupees has varied from 101 to 103 rupees Imperial. The old coins were said to contain 1¼ per cent. of alloy.

Before the days of Sirdar Singh the copper coins were very poorly struck, they also varied a good deal in weight; they were not issued from the same mint as the silver coins. The copper coins of Sirdar

[1] Page 53.

and Dúnga Singh are very fairly stamped, and those of the present Mahárájá are the best executed copper coins in Rájputána. The two copper coins of Gaj Singh, Súrut Singh, and Ratan Singh, were supposed to weigh 14 máshas and 7 máshas respectively, the coins of Sirdar Singh, Dúnga Singh, and the present Chief weigh 7 máshas. In 1890 a copper coin of 5 máshas was issued in the name of the present Mahárájá, a minor. The coins of 14 máshas are of the value of 4 pai Imperial, those of 7 máshas are worth 2 pai.

The coins of both metals are called by the name of the Mahárájá, the word Sháhí, and the value of the coin being added.

The following remarks describe the way in which the mint was regulated at Bíkaner in the year 1890, they will also suffice to give an insight as to the way in which the mints are worked throughout Rájputána.

The Durbár does not issue coins, but merely keeps the "Sikka" or die. When the sohukars (merchants), or other people, wish to have coins manufactured, they bring their metals to the Durbar mint, first getting the silver purified. For every rupee 10¼ máshas of silver has to be provided, and as the rupee weighs only 10 máshas, there is a saving of 25 máshas of silver in every 100 rupees. The 25 máshas are worth Rs. 2/8, which is expended as follows:—

	R.	A.	P.
Wastage in melting, 7½ máshas, which is worth . .	0	12	0
Customs duty	1	8	9
Cleaning charges	0	2	0
Assaying	0	0	11
Making silver sheets and cutting into proper weight	0	0	3
Weighing charges	0	0	1
	2	8	0

No alloy is mixed with the silver, because the metal of which the coins are made is not quite pure. Once, some five years ago, when the rupees were made of quite pure silver, alloy to the extent of 35½ rupees per cent. was mixed with it.

Copper is procured from Calcutta duly melted, and therefore no alloy is mixed with it. A maund of copper costs 32r. 13a. The cost of manufacturing the copper money from a maund is as follows:—

	R.	A.	P.
Cutting the copper in suitable pieces. . .	0	2	0
Making the sheets	2	4	0
Forming the coins	5	13	6
Waste	1	2	0
Stamping	0	7	3
Wages of Coolies	0	0	9
Weighing	0	5	3
Cutting a die (one die makes 6,000 coins).	0	4	0
Miscellaneous expenses on account of ganny bags, twine, paper, etc.	0	1	0
	10	7	9
Total.	43	4	9

While the cost of thus converting a maund of metal into coins is 43r. 4a. 9p. + 1r. 5a. 3p. for Customs duty, the sale proceeds amount to 50 rupees, so there is a small profit.

The new coins issued to the sohukars in 1890 are of the weight of 5 máshas, eight of these coins go to an anna. 6,400 coins of this weight are made from one maund of copper, and 5 lakhs and 60,000 coins were manufactured during the year.

Whether coins are made or not, the permanent mint establishment is as follows:—

One Hawaldár.	15	rupees per month.
One Gumáshta.	10	,,
One Engraver	7	,,
One Chaprásí	4	,,
One Weigher	2	,,
	38	,,

When the mint is working a Store-keeper at 10 rupees a month is also entertained.

On the 8th of March, 1891, Mr. C. S. Bayley, the Political Agent, wrote to me as follows: "Our coins will soon be a thing of the past, for negociations are going on by virtue of which we shall begin to use Government rupees like those made for Alwar. The railway almost makes this change necessary."

SILVER COINAGE

1. Gaj Singh's rupee. See Plate VI. figs. 1 and 8.

Obverse. سکه مبارک صاحب قران ثاني شاه عالم بادشاه غازي ۲۷

Sikka mubárak sáhib kirán sány Sháh 'Alam bádsháh ghází.

"27" in Persian numerals.

"Auspicious coin of the 2nd sáhib kirán (lord of the fortunate conjunction of the planets), the victorious Emperor Sháh 'Alam, 27."

Symbol. 

Reverse. سنة ۱۱۲۱ جلوس میمنت مانوس

Sanah 1121 *julús maimanat mánús.*

"In the fortunate year of his reign, the year A.H. 1121."

Symbols. Patáká, and circles of dots.

Weight (of my specimen). 176 grains.

2. Gaj Singh's ordinary coins. See Plate VI. fig. 12.

Obverse. سکه مبارک بادشاه غازي عالم شاه

Sikka mubárak bádsháh ghází Shah 'Alam.

"Auspicious coin of the victorious Emperor Sháh 'Alam."

Symbol.  over *ghází.*

Reverse. سنة جلوس میمنت مانوس

Sanah julús maimanat mánus.

"In the year of his fortunate reign."

The Persian character very badly executed.

Symbols. , , , ⊙ and circles of dots.

Weight. 172 grains.

3. Súrut Singh's nazr rupee. See Plate VI. figs. 2 and 8.

Obverse. The same as in No. 1.

Reverse. The same as in No. 1.

The *sanah* badly executed, 114 (?) on my specimen, which is a fine one.

Symbols. The *trisúl* and circles of dots.

Weight. 174 grains.

4. Súrut Singh's ordinary coins. See Plate VI. fig. 13.

Obverse. As in No. 2.

Reverse. As in No. 2.

Symbols. , ⊙, , circles of dots, and .

Weight. 174½ grains.

5. Ratan Singh's nazr rupee. See Plate VI. figs. 3 and 8.

Obverse. As in No. 1.

Reverse. As in No. 1.

In Persian figures 1124 instead of 1121.

Symbols. Kirnia and circles of dots.

Weight. 177 grains.

6. Ratan Singh's ordinary coins. See Plate VI. fig. 14.

Obverse. As in No. 2.

Reverse. As in No. 2.

Symbols. As in Nos. 2 and 4, with the kirnia.

Weight of the rupee, 174½ grains.

7. Sirdar Singh's nazr and ordinary coins. Type *A*. See Plate VI. figs. 5 and 5 *A*.

Obverse. مبارک بادشاه غازي عالم ۱۲۲۹

Mubárak bádsháh ghází 'Álam 1229 (?).

"Auspicious, the victorious Emperor 'Álam."

Symbol. 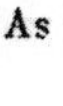

Reverse. As in No. 1, but very badly stamped.

Symbols. The patáká, kirnia, chhátá, a snake ("nág"), circles plain and of dots, and the trisúl.

Weight. 175 grains.

8. Sirdar Singh's nazr and ordinary rupees. Type *B*. See Plate VI. figs. 4, 9, and 15, and for sizes of smaller pieces figs. 16, 17, and 18.

Obverse. اورنگ اراي هند و انگلستان كوين وكتوريه ۱۸۵۹

Aurang árái Hind wa Inglistán Queen Victoria, 1859.

"Queen Victoria, the ornament of the thrones of India and England, 1859" (the date of the Proclamation).

Reverse. ضرب سري بيكنير ۱۹۱۶

Zarab sri Bikaner 1916.

Assayers marks, "۲۵," "۲۱," on each side of the *Zr* of *Zarab*.

Symbols. The marks of the former Chiefs, and the chhátá.

Weight. 175–6 grains.

9. Dúnga Singh's coins, nazr and ordinary. See Plate VI. figs. 6 and 9.

Obverse. As in No. 8.

Reverse. As in No. 8.

Symbols. Those of the four former chiefs, and the chaurí. Assayer's marks as in No. 8.

10. Ganga Singh's coins, nazr and ordinary. See Plate VI. figs. 7 and 10.

Obverse. As in No. 8.

Reverse. As in No. 8, but the date "1944" (A.D. 1887) in Persian numerals instead of the assayer's marks.

Symbols. Those of the five former Chiefs, and the morchhal.

Weight. 175 grains.

COPPER COINAGE

1. Gaj Singh's coins.

Inscription. The same as on silver coin No. 2.

Weight. 115 grains.

2. Súrut Singh's coins. See Plate VI. fig. 11.

Inscription. The same as on silver coin No. 2.

Weight. 113 grains.

3. Ratan Singh's coins.

Inscription. As on No. 2.

Weight. 117 grains.

4. Sirdar Singh's coins.

Inscription. As on No. 8.

Weight. 116 grains.

5. Dúnga Singh's coins.

Inscription. As on No. 8, and symbols as on No. 9.

Weight. 121 grains.

6. Ganga Singh's coin.

Inscription. As on No. 8 silver coins, and symbols as on No. 10 silver coins.

Weight. 122 grains.

TABLE SHOWING THE AMOUNT OF SILVER COINS STRUCK IN THE LAST FIVE YEARS

Samvat	Rupees	8 Anna	4 Anna	2 Anna
1943	44,342	....	....	....
1944	60,798	3,966	....	....
1945	29,602	....	....	....
1946	171,740	3,774	588	....
1947	24,350	....	21,020	184
(A.D. 1890.)				

KISHANGARH CURRENCIES

KISHANGARH

Area, 874 square miles. Population (in 1891), 125,516, or 144 persons per square mile. Revenue, about £27,500 a year.

This State was founded by Kishan, the ninth son of Udaya "the fat," Rájá of Márwár, in Samvat 1669 (A.D. 1612-13).

Kishan Singh was made an independent Rájá in the town which he had founded, for the iniquitous service of assassinating Govindás, a Rájput of the Bhátti tribe, one of the foreign nobles of Marú, and the confidential adviser of the then Rájá of Márwár. The murder took place in the time of Jehángír, and was at the instigation of Prince Khúrom, the second son of the Emperor by a Kachwáha princess of Ambér.

THE MINT

The mint is said, by the officials of the State, to have been established when the State was founded, but this is most unlikely. The coin with the inscription to Sháh 'Álam was probably the first to be made. The money is current throughout Kishangarh, and in the early part of this century was largely used in the Ajmere district.

GOLD COINAGE

The gold muhr weighs 11 máshas 2¼ rattis. The gold is said to be quite pure. The coin is half a ratti heavier than the Jaipur muhr. (The Kishangarh másha is only 6 rattis.) The muhrs of the State are not coined in any great number I believe, and are very rarely met with.

The coins bear the same inscription as the rupee of the same date.

SILVER COINAGE

The rupee is the only silver coin made. Its weight is said to be 11 máshas 2¼ rattis, of which 2 máshas are alloy.

1. Coin struck in the name of Sháh 'Alam.

INSCRIPTION.

Obverse. سکه مبارک بادشاه غازي شاه عالم

Sikka mubárak bádsháh ghází Sháh 'Alam.

"Auspicious coin of the victorious Emperor Sháh 'Alam."

Symbol. A jháṛ of this pattern , four leaves on the one side and four balls on the other.

Reverse. ضرب سنة جلوس ميمنت مانوس

Zarab sanah .... julús maimanat mánús.

"Struck in the .... year of his fortunate reign."

2. The Chandorí rupee. This rupee was struck out of respect to Chand Kanwar Bai, sister to Mahárána Bhím Singh of Mewár, in the early part of this century. The coin was introduced for charitable purposes. It is of exactly the same pattern as the Mewár Chandorí rupee of the second issue, except that the dies are more roughly cut, and consequently the lines on the coins appear broader. See Plate II. fig. 1.

Weight. 166 grains.

Value. Twelve annas and six pies Udaipurí, or rather less than the value of the Udaipur rupee (three pies and some pice less), see pages 10 and 11.

3. The present coin, which bears in Persian character the following inscription:—

Obverse. "In the fortunate year (1858) of the reign of Her Majesty Queen Victoria of England."

Reverse. "Coined in the 24th year of the august accession of His Highness Rájá Pirthí Singh bahádur."

Weight. 11 máshas 2¼ rattis.

Assay. Two máshas of alloy in each coin.

JAIPUR CURRENCIES

JAIPUR PLATE VII

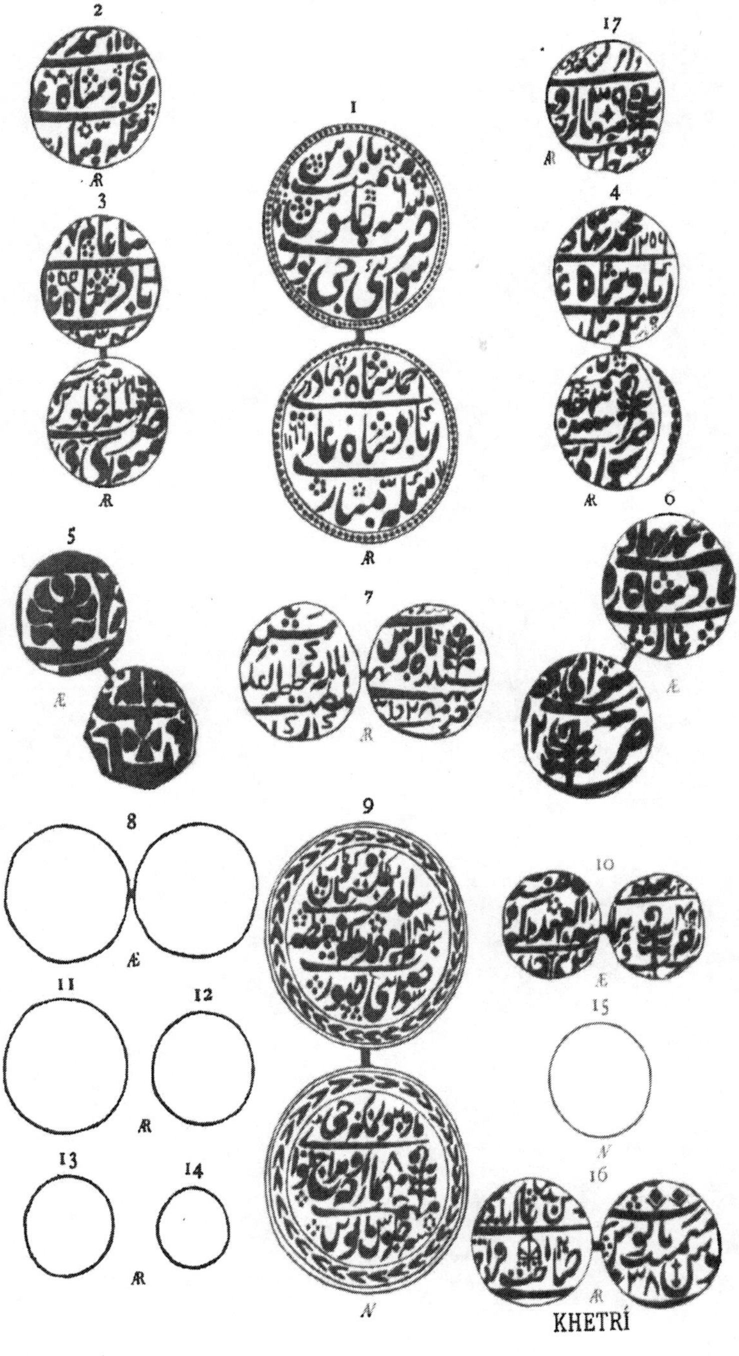

KHETRÍ

JAIPUR OR DHUNDAR

OLD CAPITAL AMBÉR, MODERN CAPITAL JAIPUR

The ancient name of the country ruled over by the Kachwáha princes is Dhúndar, a name which originated from a once celebrated sacrificial mount (d'húnd) on the western frontier. The State is now always called Jaipur, after the famous modern capital. The Jaipur territory is about 180 miles long by 120 miles broad, and, including Shaikhawáti, occupies an area of 15,349 square miles. The population in 1891 was 2,832,276, or 184 persons per square mile. The revenue is nearly £496,000.

The name Kachwá or Kachwáha, meaning "tortoise," is one applied to the Rájputs of Ajmere. The race claims descent from Kush, the second son of Ráma, King of Koshala, whose capital was Ayodhya, the modern Oude. Kush, or one of his offspring, is said to have migrated from the parental abode, and erected the castle of Rhotas on the Soame, whence, in the lapse of several generations, another distinguished scion, Rájá Nal by name, migrated westward, and in S. 351 (A.D. 295) founded the kingdom and city of Narwár. Dholá Rai, 34th in descent from Rájá Nal, was expelled the paternal dwelling, and in S. 1023 (A.D. 967), laid the foundation of the State of Dhúndar.

The Kachwáha State of Dhúndar originated in an act of usurpation. Dhola Rai being deprived of his inheritance by his uncle, his mother donning mean apparel, put the infant into a basket and travelled westward until she reached the town of Khogong (within five miles of the modern Jaipur), then inhabited by the Mínas. The mother and her son were supported by the Mína Rájá, at first in a lowly position, but upon their rank being discovered, in a becoming manner. When the boy had attained the age of Rájput manhood (14), he was sent to Dehlí, with the Khogong tribute due to the Tüar monarch. The young Kachwáha remained at Dehlí for five years, and then conceived the plan of usurping his benefactor's authority and lands. With a few of his Rájput brethren from Dehlí, at the festival of the Dewalí, he accomplished his object, filling the tank in which the Mína Chief and his followers were bathing with their dead bodies. He married a daughter of the Prince of Ajmere.

His son conquered the country of Dhúndar, and his grandson took Ambér from the head of the Mína confederation.

Pujún, who was sixth in descent from the exile of Narwar, was deemed of sufficient consequence to obtain the sister of Prithiráj of Dehlí in marriage. He was one of the sixty-four Chiefs who, with a chosen body of their retainers, enabled Prithiráj to carry off the Princess of Kanauj.

Báhár Mal was the first prince of Ambér who paid homage to the Muhammadan power. He attended the fortunes of Bábar, and received from Humáyún the munsub of "5,000," as Rájá of Ambér.

Bhagwánt Das, son of Báhár Mal, became still more intimately allied with the Mughal dynasty; he was the friend of Akbar. His name is execrated in Rájputána, as the first[1] of her princes who lowered the honour of the Rájpúts by forming a matrimonial alliance with the Islamite. His daughter was married to Prince Selim, afterwards the Emperor Jehángír.

Jai Singh II., who is better known by the title of "Sawai Jai Singh" (the term "Sawai" meaning "raised above all other princes"), succeeded to the Ambér gaddí in S. 1755 (A.D. 1698). He was a great statesman, legislator, and man of science. He laid the foundations of Jaipur, the modern capital, in S. 1784 (A.D. 1728). The new town became the seat of science and art, and eclipsed the glories of Ambér, with which the fortifications of the modern city unite, although the extremity of the one is six miles from the other. Jai Singh was an ardent astronomer; he erected observatories and furnished them with instruments of his own invention, and obtained results which were so correct as to astonish the most learned.[2] The Kachwáha State owes everything to Jai Singh; before his time it had little political weight beyond that which it ac-

[1] It is stated by some writers that Báhár Mal had previously given a daughter in marriage to Akbar.

[2] It is a fact not generally known that a portion of the credit for these correct observations and astronomical labours generally, given in all Histories and Chronicles, English and Indian, to the unaided genius of the Great Maháráját, ought to be given to a German, the Roman Priest Father Andreas Strobl, S.J., who had been sent for (before 1739, and who died at Agrah on the 30th March, 1751) with another savant from Germany by the Astronomer Rájá of Jaipur. I state this on the authority of Tieffentaller (Vol. i. of the 1785 Berlin edition of his *Beschreibung von Hindustan*, p. 4), who visited Father Strobl shortly before his death. Tieffentaller was then living in the fort of Narwár, and his words are:—"Bey meinem zwölfjährigen Aufenthalt zu Narvar habe ich drey bis viermal zu Agra und Dehli den würdigen Pater Andreas Strobel besucht, den der Zeporische König Zesing, ein grosser Liebhaber der astronomie, nebst noch einem andern Manne aus Deutschland berufen hatte.

quired from the personal character of its princes, and the estimation in which they were held at the Mughal Court. Notwithstanding the intimate connection which existed between the Ambér Rájás and the Imperial family from the time of Bábar to that of Aurungzeb, their patrimonial estates had been very little enlarged since the time of Pujún, the contemporary of the last Rájput Emperor of Dehlí. It was not till the troubles which ensued on the demise of Aurungzeb, when the Empire was partitioned, that Jaipur was entitled to the name of a Ráj. During those troubles, Jai Singh, as the Emperor's lieutenant in Ágrah, had ample opportunity to enlarge and consolidate his territory.

Isvari (Eesuri) Singh succeeded to a well-defined territory, a full treasury, and an efficient army. According to the fixed law of primogeniture he was the proper successor to Jai Singh; but Mádhu Singh, a younger son, born of a princess of Mewár, possessed conventional rights which vitiated those of birth. By the help of the Maháráná of Mewár, who bought for him the aid of Holkar, Mádhu Singh gained the throne.

Jaipur accepted the protection of the British Government in 1818. On the 2nd of April of that year the treaty was concluded which made the Kachwáha princes the friends and tributaries in perpetuity of Great Britain.

LIST OF JAIPUR CHIEFS FROM A.D. 1698 TO DATE

	Name	Date of ascending the gaddi	Date of death
1.	Mahárájá Sawái Jai Singh	1699	1743
2.	,, Isvari (Eesuri) Singh	1743	1760
3.	,, Mádhu Singh	1760	1778
4.	,, Prithi Singh II.	1778	1778
5.	,, Pratáp Singh	1778	1803
6.	,, Jagat Singh II.	1803	1818
7.	,, Mohan Singh[1]	1818	1819
8.	,, Jai Singh III.[2]	1819, April 25th, the day of his birth	1835
9.	,, Rám Singh	1835	1880
10.	,, Mádho Singh	1880	Now living.

[1] Son of Manohara Singh, ex-Rájá of Narwár, and 15th in descent from Prithiráj the 1st of Ambér. He was raised to the gaddí, but removed on the birth of Jai Singh, a son of the late Chief by the Bhattiani Queen.

[2] A posthumous son.

THE MINTS

It is stated by the Jaipur officials, that a mint was worked at Ambér prior to the foundation of Jaipur. The probability is that this statement is incorrect (unless it applies only to very early times), for Ambér was a small State and early came under Moslem sway. The State officials reported to Captain, now Sir Edward, Bradford, in the early part of the year 1870, that the Ambér mint was closed, and the Jaipur-town mint opened on the foundation of the new capital by Jai Singh in 1728, but this report must be received in a very guarded manner. I have sought for, and asked the Jaipur officials for specimens of Jai Singh's coins with a negative result, and I do not believe he ever was allowed to coin. The earliest coins of the State I have met with are those of Isvari Singh, A.D. 1743–1760, and even these are early coins for a Rájput State. It is probable that Jaipur was amongst the first of the States allowed to set up an independent mint, the privilege being perhaps early gained in consequence of the very close relationship existing between the Chief and his Suzerain at Dehlí.

In addition to the Jaipur-town mint, mints have, during this century, been worked at Máhdúpur, Jíkur, Bupas, Súrujghar, and Charána in Khetrí, the two latter were closed in the year 1869, the others at an earlier but now unknown date.

In 1802–3, the revenue from the Jaipur mint was reported to be about 60,000 rupees a year.

The special mint-mark of the State is a "Jháṛ" of six sprigs or branches. The accompanying figure represents an old mint-mark given by Prinsep,[1] and was seen by him on both muhrs and rupees.

The coins of the State are called the "Jháṛ Sáhí."

GOLD COINAGE

I do not know at what date gold was first coined, but possibly it was struck from the date of the opening of the mint. The only gold coins which I have been able to obtain are those of Rám Singh and the

[1] Page 43.

present Maháráјá, but earlier coins existed. The gold muhrs are coined in large quantities, and are freely circulated in Rájputána, and amongst the native community in more distant parts of India.

Both nazr and ordinary muhrs are at present coined.

1. Muhr struck at Jainagar (another name for Jaipur), mentioned in Prinsep's *Tables*,[1] as weighing 174.99 grains, and as having 164.05 grains of pure contents.

2. Jaipur muhrs the weights of which are given by Prinsep.[2] These were coined anterior to Ram Singh's time.[3]

3. Muhr of Rám Singh. (1837–1880.)

INSCRIPTION.

Obverse. ضرب سواي جيپور سنة ١٨٦٨ بعهد ملكه معظمه سلطنت انگلستان وكتوريه

Zarab sawái Jaipur sanah 1868 *ba-ahdi malikah mu'azzamah Sultanat Inglistán Victoria.*

"Struck at Sawai Jaipur in the year 1868, by permission of Her Majesty Victoria Queen of England."

Reverse. سنة ٣١ جلوس ميمنت مانوس مهاراوراج سواي رام سنگه جي

Sanah 31 *julús maimanat mánús Maháráo-ráj Sawai Rám Singhjí.*

"In the 31st year of the fortunate reign of Mahárão-ráj Rám Singh."

Symbol. A six-branched jháṛ.

Weight. 167½ grains.

The gold is stated to be quite pure.

[1] Page 43.

[2] *Op. cit.* p. 51.

[3] The gold muhr of the State is said by the officials to have always been of the same weight, and its gold quite pure, but in the Government Assay Tables as many as six "Jaipur" muhrs are shown, differing in weight and in other respects. The following is a list of these muhrs extracted from the Assay Tables:—

Name	Weight in grains	Assay in car. grains	Touch of gold in 100 parts	Pure contents in grains
Jaipur, sanah 8	166.60	W. 20	100	138.83
,, ,, 22	168.11	B. 20	100	168.11
,, ,, 23	167.94	B. 20	100	167.94
,, ,, 24	168.12	B. 20	100	168.12
,, various sanát	167.80	B. 20	100	167.80
,, Sawái, sanah 18	168.10	B. 13¼	99.2	166.79

The above are averages of many (all new) coins from the Jaipur mint.

4. Muhr of the present Chief.

Inscription exactly the same as that on Rám Singh's coin, with the substitution of Mádho Singh's name for that of Rám Singh.

See Plate VII. fig. 9 for the nazr muhr, and fig. 15 for the sizes of the ordinary muhrs of Rám and Mádho Singh.

SILVER COINAGE

The silver coins are the rupee, eight-anna, four-anna and two-anna bits. Both nazr and ordinary rupees are coined.

1. Coin of A.H. 1156 (A.D. 1743). See Plate VII. fig. 2. This was struck by Isvari Singh, either in the name of Sultán Muhammad Ibráhím (A.D. 1719), or, what is more likely, in that of Muhammad Sháh Abul Fath Násir-ad-dín (A.D. 1719–1748).

INSCRIPTION.

Obverse. سکه مبارک بادشاه غازي محمد شاه ۱۱۵۶

Sikka mubárak bádsháh ghází Muhammad Sháh, 1156.

"Auspicious coin of the victorious Emperor Muhammad Sháh, 1156."

Symbols. Circles of dots.

Reverse. ضرب سواي جيپور سنة ۲۹ جلوس ميمنت مانوس

Zarab Sawái Jaipur sanah 29 *julús maimanat mánús.*

"Struck at Sawai Jaipur in the 29th year of his fortunate reign."

Symbols. Circles of dots.

Weight. 175 grains.

2. Isvari Singh's rupee struck in the name of Ahmad Sháh. See Plate VII. fig. 1.

INSCRIPTION.

Obverse. سکه مبارک بادشاه غازي احمد شاه بهادر ۱۱۶۶

Sikka mubárak bádsháh ghází Ahmad Sháh bahádur, 1166.

"Auspicious coin of the victorious Emperor Ahmad Sháh, 1166."

Reverse. ضرب سواي جيپور سنة ۶ جلوس ميمنت مانوس

Zarab Sawái Jaipur sanah 6 *julús maimanat mánús.*

"Struck at Sawái Jaipur in the 6th year of his fortunate reign."

Symbols. Circles of dots on both surfaces.

Weight. 175 grains.

3. Mádhu Singh's coins. Called the "Mádhurghev bádsháhí rupee, etc." See Plate VII., fig. 3. A.D. 1760–1778.

INSCRIPTION.

Obverse. سکه مبارک بادشاه غازي شاه عالم بهادر

Sikka mubárak bádsháh ghází Sháh 'Álam bahádur.

"Auspicious coin of the victorious monarch Sháh 'Álam."

Symbols. Circles of dots, and this mark 

Reverse. ضرب سواي جيپور سنة ٣٤ جلوس ميمنت مانوس

Zarab Sawáí Jaipur sanah 34 *julús maimanat mánús.*

"Struck at Jaipur in the 34th year of his fortunate reign."

Symbol. The jháṛ.

Weight. 175 grains.

4. Jagat Singh's coins. He probably continued to strike coin from the same die as that from which the last-mentioned coin was stamped; there is, however, one special coin of his known. Jagat Singh enjoyed the reputation of being the most dissolute prince of his age; the most celebrated of his concubines was an Islamite, "*Ras Kaphúr*" ("the essence of camphor") by name. Tod states that in this woman's name and honour the Chief struck coin, he installed her as queen of half his dominions, and actually conveyed to her in gift a moiety of the personalty of the crown. I have been unable to procure a specimen of this unique issue.

5. Coins struck by Rám Singh in the name of Muhammad Sháh. See Plate VII. fig. 4.

Struck in A.H. 1256 (A.D. 1840).

Obverse. سکه مبارک بادشاه غازي محمد شاه بهادر ١٢٥٦

Sikka mubárak bádsháh ghází Muhammad Sháh bahádur, 1256.

"Auspicious coin of the victorious Emperor Muhammad Sháh, A.H. 1256."

Reverse. ضرب سواي جيپور سنة ٣ جلوس ميمنت مانوس

Zarab Sawái Jaipur sanah 3 *julús maimanat mánús.*

"Struck at Sawái Jaipur in the 3rd year of his fortunate reign."

Symbols. The jháṛ and a circle of dots. Sanah 3 probably refers to the 3rd year of Rám Singh's reign, in which case he ascended the gaddí in A.D. 1837, and not in 1835 as stated in the Table at p. 73.

Weight. 175 grains.

6. Rupee weighing 167 grains. Coined at one of the local mints (?). See Plate VII. fig. 7.

INSCRIPTION.

Obverse. سكه مبارك سلطنت ملكه معظمه انگلستان و هندوستان ؟

Sikka mubárak sultanat malikah mu'azzamah Inglistán wa Hindústán?

Reverse. ضرب جلوس ميمنت مانوس

Zarab julús maimanat mánús.

"Struck in his fortunate reign."

Symbol. The jháṛ.

7. Rám Singh's coins, 1860–1879.

Inscription. The same as on Rám Singh's gold muhr. See page 75.

Symbols. Obverse, a circle of dots. Reverse, the jháṛ, and this mark ✦

Weight. 175 grains.

8. Coins of H.H. Mádho Singh, A.D. 1879 to date. The coins of the current year are called "Hálí coins." (*Háli* means "the present one.")

Inscription. The same as on the last coin, substituting "Mádho Singhjí" for "Rám Singhjí."

Symbols. Obverse, a circle of dots. Reverse, a jháṛ.

Weight. 175 grains for the rupee, and for the smaller pieces in exact proportion. (For the sizes of the silver pieces see Plate VII. figs. 11, 12, 13, and 14. For the nazr rupee see the same Plate, fig. 9, but in silver.)

In Prinsep's *Useful Tables*, p. 56, the weight of the Jaipur rupee is given as 174 grains, its assay as Br. 12, its "touch" as 96.7, and its pure contents as 168.20. The intrinsic value of 100 rupees is stated to be 101.939 Imperial coins.

COPPER COINAGE

1. Old Jháṛ Sáhí. See Plate VII. fig. 5. Struck in the name of Sháh 'Álam. This coin is said to have been struck about the year 1760; it is still current in the Jaipur State, and also in a large amount about Bhílwárrá in Mewár.

INSCRIPTION.

Obverse. سکه مبارک بادشاه غازي شاه عالم

Sikka mubárak bádshdh ghási Sháh 'Álam.

"Auspicious coin of the victorious Emperor Sháh 'Álam."

Symbol. A cross made by triangular-shaped dots above the word "Sháh."

Reverse. ضرب سواي جيپور

Zarab Sawái Jaipur.

"Struck at Sawái Jaipur."

Symbol. A jháṛ.

Weight. 262 grains.

2. Coin struck between the years 1786 and 1806, in the name of Muhammad Sháh. See Plate VII. fig. 6. This is the coin Prinsep (*Tables*, p. 63) describes as weighing 280 grains; in his day (*circa* 1830) the exchange rate of this coin was 35 to the rupee; it was then in circulation in the Jaipur and Ágrah districts.

INSCRIPTION.

Obverse. سکه مبارک بادشاه غازي محمد شاه بهادر

Sikka mubárak bádshdh ghási Muhammad Sháh bahádur.

"Auspicious coin of the victorious Emperor Muhammad Sháh bahádur."

Reverse. ضرب سنة ١٢ سواي جيپور

Zarab sanah 12 Sawái Jaipur.

"Struck at Sawái Jaipur in the 12th year."

Symbols. A jháṛ and a fish.

Weight. About 282 grains.

3. Copper coin of Rám Singh. See Plate VII. fig. 10, and fig. 8 for the size of a paisá of the same description, which latter was introduced when Rám Singh's dies were first cut.

Inscription. The same as on Rám Singh's other coins.

Weight. 94–96 grains.

In 1870, Captain, now Sir Edward, Bradford reported to the Agent to the Governor-General for Rájputána that the copper mint, though still existing, had not been worked for many years owing to the depreciation in the value of the Jaipur copper money. Soon after this report the issue of copper money was resumed, for I possess a Jaipur paisá of the year 1874, the 40th year of Rám Singh's reign, its weight is 96 grains.

4. Copper coins of Mádho Singh. They are like those of Rám Singh, the name having been duly altered.

JAIPUR FEUDATORIES

KHETRÍ

The Khetrí State lies in the north of Shaikhawátí, and its Rájá is one of the principal Chiefs in the Confederation. He is descended from Balojí, the third son of Rájá Udayakarna, who succeeded to the gaddí of Ambér in S. 1445 (A.D. 1389). Fourth in descent from Balojí was Shaikhjí, who received his name in compliment to a miracle-working Muhammadan Saint to whose prayers the childless Chief was supposed to be indebted for the birth of his son. Shaikhjí became the ancestor of a numerous race, who under the name of Shaikhawut, occupy an important part of Rájputána, nearly 10,000 miles in area. Shaikhjí threw off the control of the Ambér princes, and discontinued the tribute, making the Shaikhawut colonies distinct from the parent State. The Shaikhawuts, however, are now tributary to Jaipur; this supremacy of Ambér over the Confederated States recommenced in the time of Jai Singh II. (1699–1743).

The Khetrí family belongs to the tribe of Sádhanís or Chieftans of northern Shaikhawátí. The Sádhanís are descended from Bhojráj, the third son of Rayasil, the first Rájá amongst the sons of Shaikhjí. His descendant, Sádhu, wrested Khetrí and its dependencies from the Tüars, and his offspring assuming their father's name as a patronymic are called Sádhaní. The rent-roll of the State is said to be about £45,000 a year.

THE MINT

The mint has not been worked since the year A.D. 1869. Gold was not coined in this State.

SILVER COINAGE

The only coin of this State which I have been able to procure is the one struck in the name of Muhammad Sháh 'Álam. It was introduced into circulation between the years 1759 and 1786. See Plate VII. fig. 16.

INSCRIPTION.

Obverse. سکه صاحب قران زد زتائید الله حامي دين محمد شاه
عالم بادشاه ١٢

Sikka sáhib kirán zad zataede Allah hámi-ad-dín Muhammad Sháh 'Alam bádsháh, 12.

"By the help of God, the defender of the religion of Muhammad, Sháh 'Alam the king struck coin as the Sáhib kirán, 12."

Symbol. above the *hb* of *sáhib* (the Chhátá or umbrella).

Reverse. سنة ٣٨ جلوس ميمنت مانوس ضرب

Sanah 38 *julús maimanat mánús zarab* (*Khetrí?*).

"Struck at (Khetrí?) in the 38th year of his fortunate reign."

Symbols. above the *b* of the word *zarab* and by the side of the 3 of the 38. This mark in the curl of the *s* of *julús*.

COPPER COINAGE

In Prinsep's *Useful Tables*[1] a copper coin weighing 252 grains is mentioned.

[1] Page 63.

BÚNDÍ CURRENCIES

BÚNDÍ

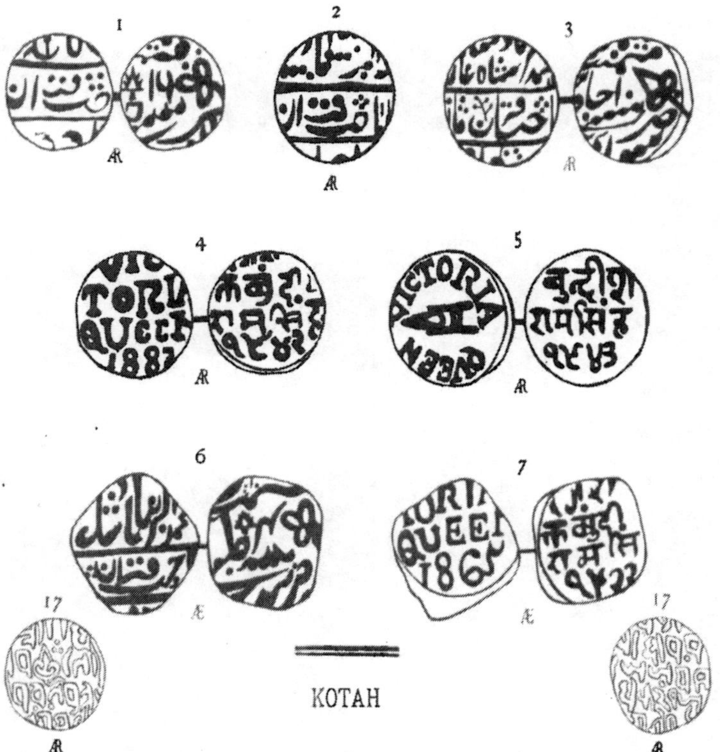

KOTAH

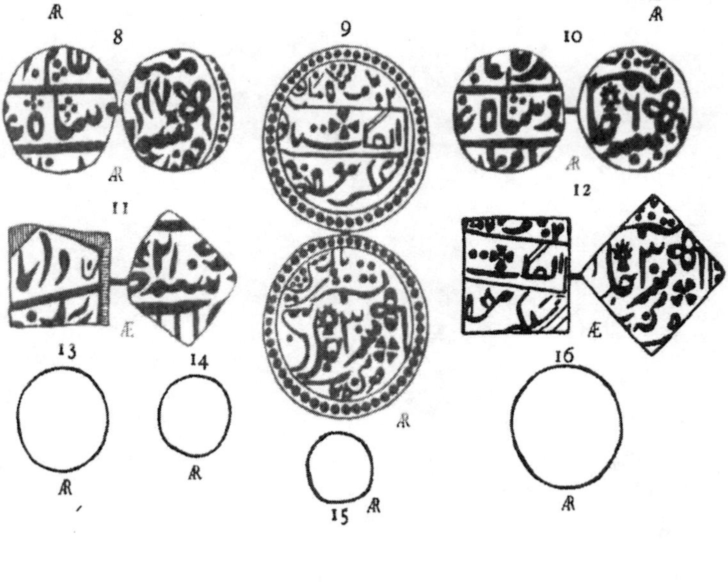

BUNDI

CAPITAL BUNDI

The area of this State is 2,225 square miles. The population, in 1891, was 295,675, or 133 persons per square mile. The revenue is about £60,000 a year.

Búndí is one of the States comprehended by the name "Haráotí," "the country of the Hárás," the other State being Kotah. The Chumbul separates these countries from one another. The Hárás are one of the most important of the 24 Chohan Sác'há; they descend from Anúráj, son of Manik Rai, king of Ajmere, who in A.D. 685 sustained the first shock of the Islamite arms. The Chohans were one of the most illustrious of the 36 royal races of India.

In A.D. 1342, Rao Deva took the Bandú valley from the Mínas, founded the city of Búndí, and styled the country Hárávatí or Haráotí. For a long period Búndí was in some respects subject to Mewár, but Rao Súrjun, who succeeded to the gaddí in A.D. 1533, received a magnificent bribe from Akbar to throw off the remnant of his allegiance to Mewár, and to follow the victorious car of the Mughal. Akbar granted to the Chief the title of "Ráo Rájá of Búndí." The partition of the country into the two States of Búndí and Kotah, took place in the early part of the seventeenth century, Kotah being granted to Mádhu Singh, the second son of the Ráo Rájá. Búndí was one of the first Rájput States to form an alliance with the British Government; Major Tod conducted the treaty in the February of 1818.

THE MINT

The officials of the State say that the mint has existed from time immemorial, but I have been unable to find any Búndí coins of an earlier date than Sháh 'Álam's time. No gold coins have been struck. The rupee of the year is known as the "Hálí" rupee (present one). The *Gárah sanah* rupee, or rupee of the 11th year, has *Sanah* 11 stamped on it; this rupee is used chiefly for charitable purposes, weddings, etc.;

as it is of less value than the Hálí coin a small sum is saved by its use, while an equally good name for liberality is obtained. In a letter from the Political Agent at the Court to the Agent to the Governor-General for Rájputána, dated April 18th, 1870, No. 29, F, it is stated that both the *Háli* rupee and the *Gárah sanah* weighed 11¾ máshas. The Hálí coin is reported to have contained ½ a másha of alloy, while the Gárah sanah contained one másha of alloy.

In 1819, Mr. Wilder, the Political Agent at Ajmere, reported to Government that the Búndí rupee was current in Ajmere, and that a debased Búndí rupee was in circulation about Ujjain. By the Assay Tables it appears that the coinage was reformed in 1825.

BUNDI COINS FROM PRINSEP'S TABLES[1]

Name	Weight	Pure contents	Value of 100
Rupee of 1819	171.56	152.26	92.273
Rupee of 1825	172.82	163.46	98.62

SILVER COINAGE

1. The old Hálí rupee, said to have been coined early in the time of Sháh 'Alam (A.D. 1759–1786), but still in circulation. See Plate VIII. fig. 1.

INSCRIPTION.

Obverse. سکه مبارک صاحب قران ثاني شاه عالم

Sikka mubárak sáhib kirán sány Sháh 'Alam.

"Auspicious coin of Sháh 'Alam, the second Sáhib kirán (lord of the fortunate conjunction of planets)."

Reverse. ضرب .... سنة ١٦ جلوس ميمنت مانوس

Zarab .... (?) *sanah* 16 (and others) *julús maimanat mánús.*

"Struck at .... in the 16th year of his fortunate reign."

Symbols. A triple bow and a flower

Value. 16 annas Imperial.

Weight 171 grains.

[1] page 53

2. Búndí rupee struck in the name of Akbar Sháh II. Struck after the year 1806 and up to the year 1859. See Plate VIII. fig. 3.

INSCRIPTION.

Obverse. سكه مبارك صاحب قران ثاني محمد اكبر شاه بادشاه غازي

Sikka mubárak sáhib kirán sány Muhammad Akbar Sháh bádsháh ghází.

"Auspicious coin of the second *sáhib kirán* (lord of the fortunate conjunction of planets), the noble monarch Muhammad Akbar the king."

Reverse.

Zarab sawái Búndish (?) *sanah* 10 (and others) *julús maimanat mánús.*

"Struck at sawái Búndí in the 10th year of his fortunate reign."

Symbols. A small jháṛ over the *n* of *Kirán* on the obverse. On the reverse, a triple bow, with the central loop pointed or rounded (pointed in the coin of sanah 10).

Value. 16 annas Imperial. Weight. About 170 grains.

3. Gárah sanah rupee. See Plate VIII. fig. 2.

Inscription. As in No. 2.

Symbols. No jháṛ on the obverse; on the reverse the triple bow has a rounded central loop, and the phúllí.

Value. 14½ annas. Weight. 168 grains.

4. Rám Sháhí. These coins were first struck in 1859. See Plate VIII. fig. 4.

INSCRIPTION.

On the obverse, in English: "Victoria Queen," and the A.D. date. The English numerals are sometimes reversed (8581).

Reverse. In Nágarí—

रंगेश भक्त बुंदीश राम सिंह १८४३

Rangeça bhakta Búndiça Ráma Sinhaḥ, and the Samvat year (1843).

"The worshipper of Rangeça, the Lord of Búndí, Rám Singh."

Value. 16 annas Imperial. Weight. About 170½ grains.

5. Katár Sháhí rupee. First coined in 1886. See Plate VIII. fig. 5.

INSCRIPTION.

Obverse. In English: "Queen Victoria."

Symbol. The dagger.

Reverse. In Nágarí—

बुन्दीश राम सिंह १८४३

Búndiça Ráma Sinha, and the Samvat year, 1843.

Value. 16 annas Imperial. Weight. 165 grains.

COPPER COINAGE

1. Old Búndí coins. See Plate VIII. fig. 6.

Inscription. As in No. 2 silver coin, but with symbols as in No. 3 silver coin.

Weight. There are irregularly square, and well-fashioned circular pieces (the latter are rare) weighing 270–4 grains, and square pieces weighing 135 grains.

Value. In Prinsep's time (*circa* 1830), 32 of the larger coins went to the rupee.

2. Modern Búndí paisá, coined since 1859. See Plate VIII. fig. 7.

Inscription. As in the silver coin No. 4.

Weight. The average weight of the coins issued in A.D. 1865 is 270 grains, while that of those issued in 1877 is only 170 grains.

KOTAH CURRENCIES

KOTAH

CAPITAL KOTAH

This State has an area of 3803 square miles, a population (in 1891) of 526,267, or 138 persons per square mile, and a revenue of above £294,000 a year.

The Kotah is a junior branch of the Búndí family. Lieut.-Colonel Tod states (Annals and Antiquities of Rajast'han, Vol. ii. p. 466) that Sháh Jehán, Emperor of India, bestowed Kotah and its dependencies (a portion of the ancient Búndí kingdom), on Mádhu Singh, the second son of Ráo Ruttun of Búndí, for his distinguished gallantry in the battle of Búrhanpúr.[1]

Bhím Singh, who reigned from A.D. 1705 to 1720, was the first to bear the title of Maháráo.

The Kotah State owes its prosperity almost entirely to Zálim Singh, a Rájput of the Jhála tribe, who was for long regent and ruler (in everything but name) of the State. During the brilliant and eventful period which preceded the acknowledgment of the British as the paramount power in India, when every province from the Ganges to the ocean was agitated by warlike demonstrations, the Regent's camp was the focus of intelligence. For the important services he rendered to the British Government, the sovereignty of the four districts which he rented from Holkar was granted to him; he would, however, only accept the reward in the name of his Master, the Maháráo. Tod calls the Regent the Machiavelli of Rájast'hán.

The treaty between this State and the Government was concluded at Dehlí on December 26th, 1817, and in the March of the next year two supplemental articles were agreed to.

THE MINT

Formerly there were three Kotah mints, located at Kotah-city, Jhálra Pátan, and at Gángroun (Gágraun). In 1870 the Political Agent re-

[1] If the Kotah State were established while Sháh Jehán was Emperor, it must have been separated from Búndí after the year A.D. 1628. Various writers, however, say that this state was founded in the time of Jehángír, in or about the year 1620 or 1625.

ported to the Government that there was only one mint in the State—that at Kotah-city. The Kotah officials seem to think that the mint was established when the kingdom was founded, but this is most improbable, and I have been unable to collect any Kotah coins of an earlier date than Sháh 'Álam's time.

In 1819 Mr. Wilder reported that the Kotah rupee was current in the Ajmere district.

On August 1st, 1823, Major J. Caulfield, Agent in Haráotí, wrote as follows: "In Kotah there exists an usage that the currency should suffer a depreciation of one per cent. on the third year after its issue, and continue at that rate during the reign of the sovereign: on the accession of his successor it suffers a further annual fractional depreciation, which operates to bring the whole of the circulating medium into the mint for re-coinage."

When Prinsep wrote his book, between the years 1833 and 1838, the three mints were supposed to turn out about 36 lakhs a year, he reported that the currency had not been debased.

In 1870 gold, silver, and copper were all being coined.

The coins of the State are now pretty well confined to the Kotah district in their circulation, but formerly they were current over a much larger area.

The mark of the mint is "a triple-bow or knot," which is sometimes described as a "Jháṛ of three Pakhries." A "phúllí" or "flower" is also found on some of the coins.

In Prinsep's *Useful Tables*, p. 27, it is stated, that "at Kotá the executive authority has a shroff [banker] in each town, and participates in all the benefits arising out of money operations in the market." The currency is said not to have been debased at any period.

GOLD COINAGE

Gold was formerly coined in large amounts, and the muhrs were common coins when Prinsep wrote. Gold was also being issued in 1870. The coins are now very rarely met with; I have been unable to ascertain when specimens were last struck.

The gold coins corresponded with the rupees of the period in which they were issued and bore the same inscriptions. See Plate VIII. figs. 8, 9, and 10, but in gold.

ASSAY TABLE

Description	Weight	Pure contents in 100 parts	Pure contents in grains
Sanah 1 to 18	167.08	95.8	160.12
Sanah 19	166.72	98·2	163.68

SILVER COINAGE

1. Coin struck in the name of Sháh 'Álam. See Plate VIII. fig. 8.

INSCRIPTION.

Obverse. سکه مبارک بادشاه غازي شاه عالم بهادر

Sikka mubárak bádsháh ghází Sháh 'Álam bahádur.

"Auspicious coin of the noble monarch Sháh 'Álam bahádur."

Symbols. Four dots over the *sh* and *h* of *Bádsháh*.

Reverse. ضرب سنة جلوس ميمنت مانوس ۴۷

Zarab sanah julús maimanat mánús (sanah 47 on a specimen in my cabinet).

"Struck in the 47th year of his fortunate reign."

Symbols. The triple bow, the flower, and a small star over the word *sanah*.

Weight. 171 grains.

2. Coin struck in the name of Muhammad Bídár Bakht (1788). See Plate VIII. fig. 10.

INSCRIPTION.

Obverse. سکه مبارک بادشاه غازي محمد شاه بهادر

Sikka mubárak bádsháh ghází Muhammad Sháh bahádur.

"Auspicious coin of the victorious Emperor Muhammad Sháh bahádur."

Reverse. As in No. 1, but no small cross over the word *sanah*. The specimen in my collection is of *sanah* 6.

Weight. 175 grains.

3. Silver coins struck in the name of the Queen. They are the nazr rupee, ordinary rupee, eight-anna, four-anna, and two-anna pieces. See Plate VIII. fig. 9, and figs. 13, 14, 15, and 16 for the sizes of average coins.

INSCRIPTION.

Obverse. ضرب کوطه سنة جلوس میمنت مانوس

Zarab Kotah sanah julús maimanat mánús

"Struck at Kotah in the year of the fortunate reign of."

Symbols. The triple bow, the flower, and a cross below the bow.

Reverse. ملکه معظمه انگلستان بادشاه غازي ۲

Malikah mu'azzamah Inglistán bádshāh ghází, 2.

"Her Majesty of England, the victorious monarch, 2."

Symbol. A cross over *Inglistán*.

Weight. Of both rupees 175.8 grains (11¼ máshas), and of the smaller pieces in proportion.

Value. The same as the Imperial rupee. The coins are said to be of pure silver.

TABLE OF SILVER COINS

Description	Weight	Touch	Pure contents	Value of 100
Kotah, Old Rupee	172.65	97.3	167.97	101.803
Rupee of 1825	174.02	97.5	169.67	102.830
Present Rupee	175.8	....	....	....

COPPER COINAGE

1. Inscription as in No. 1 silver coins. See Plate VIII. fig. 11.

Weight. 275 to 278 grains.

Prinsep[1] gives the former weight (but I have specimens weighing 278 grains), and adds that the coins were current in Kotah and Ajmere, and that 34 went to a rupee.

2. A coin with the same inscription as No. 3 silver coin. See Plate VIII. fig. 12. This coin is exceedingly well struck and fashioned.

Weight. About 282 grains.

Both the above mentioned copper coins are square, the former very irregularly so.

[1] *Useful Tables*, p. 63.

JHÁLÁWÁR CURRENCIES

JHÁLÁWÁR

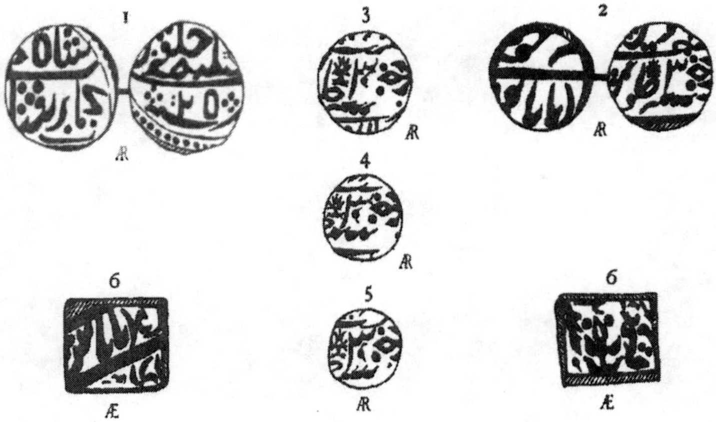

JAISALMER

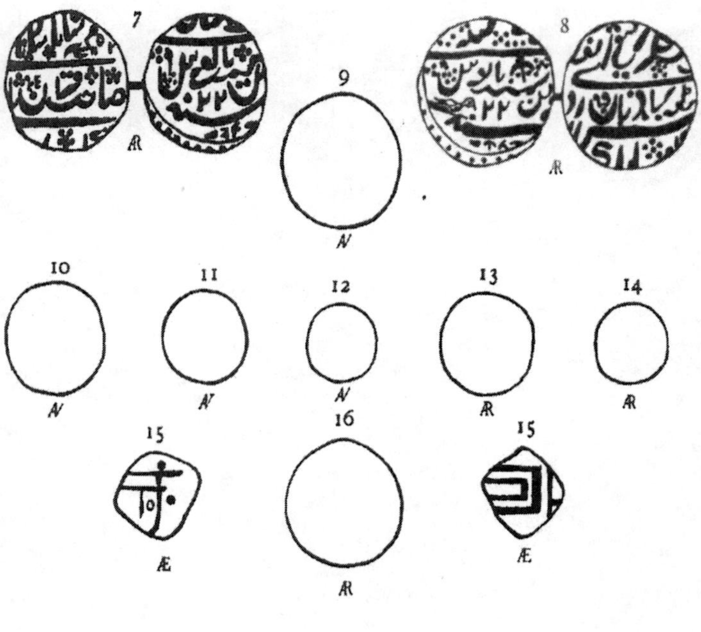

JHÁLÁWÁR

CAPITAL JHÁLRA PÁTAN

Area, 3043 square miles. Revenue, about £152,500. Population in 1891, 343,601, or 113 persons per square mile.

This state, originally a part of Kotah, was founded by Mahárúj-Rúná Madan Singh on the 8th of April, 1837. Madan Singh, a son of Mádho Singh, ascended the gaddí at Jhálra Pátan, on Baisákh Sudi the 3rd, S. 1894, or the 11th of July, A.D. 1837.

The following is a list of the Chiefs since the foundation of the kingdom to the present day:—

	Came to the Gaddi	Died
1. Mahárúj-Rúná Madan Singh.[1]	A.D. 1837, July 11th. Baisákh Sudi 3rd, S. 1894.	1847, July 1st. Asárh Badi 8th, S. 1904.
2. Mahárúj-Rúná Prithí Singh. (Legitimate son of Madan Singh.)	A.D. 1847, July 15th. Asárh Sudi 4th, S. 1904.	1875, Aug. 29th. Bhádon Badi 13, S. 1932.
3. Mahárúj-Rúná Zálim Singh. (An adopted son of Prithí Singh.)	A.D. 1877, June 15th. Asárh Badi 8th. S. 1933. (Proclaimed on the day of Prithí Singh's death.)	Now living 1892

THE MINT

In the days when Jhálawár formed part of the kingdom of Kotah, a mint, at which the coins of the latter-named State were struck, was located at Pátan. The coins from the Kotah mints were then current throughout the territory (see Kotah).

The only mint in the state is at Jhálra Pátan.

[1] Grandson of Zálim Singh the famous Kotah minister and regent, see p. 91.

GOLD COINAGE

No gold coins have ever been struck in the State.

SILVER COINAGE

The coins of the State are the rupee, eight-anna, four-anna, and two-anna pieces.

There are two distinct types of coin in circulation. The pieces of both types are known as the "Madan Sháhí," and for the sake of distinction I designate them as the "old Madan Sháhí" and the "new Madan Sháhí." The old Madan Sháhí coins were first struck in A.D. 1837, and the issue of them was continued until the end of the year 1857, when the new coins were introduced. Coins of the old pattern were issued yearly, the coins of each year being distinguished by the "sanát," which range from sanah 1 to sanah 21, corresponding with the Samvat years 1894 to 1914. The new Madan Sháhí coins were first issued after the Mutiny, in 1857. On them also the "sanah" has been regularly stamped from 1 to 34, corresponding to the years A.D. 1857 to 1891, or Samvat years 1914 to 1948. The last year, "sanah 34," since the issue of coins bearing the Queen's name, commenced on July 3rd, 1890, and terminated on July 22nd, 1891.

The pieces issued in the year then running its course are called "hálí" (the present one), to distinguish them from the Madan Sháhí coins of former years. The local names of the coins of the year are "Hálí rupee," "Hálí áṭh anni," "Hálí chou anni," and "Hálí do anni." The rupee of the year just passed is called "summeh ka rupia." These names were introduced in the times when any rupee or coin of the State, save those issued in the current year, were charged with a "butta" or "exchange rate." The custom of butta, now abolished, caused the coins to be returned yearly to the mint for re-stamping, a process which was a considerable source of revenue to the State. The highest butta ever charged is said to have been 12 annas per cent.

In consequence of the custom of butta, it is very difficult to obtain specimens of the earlier issues.

Both the old and the new Madan Sháhí coins bear only parts of the inscriptions found on the dies, and all the pieces of different values in an issue are, and were always, struck from a stamp or die of the same magnitude. The dies were and are very roughly cut, and the coins of the State are very poor.

1. The old Madan Sháhí coins (1837 to 1857) bear the following inscription (see Plate IX. fig. 1) in the Persian character:

Obverse. سکه مبارک بادشاه غازي محمد شاه بهادر

Sikka Mubárak bádsháh ghází Muhammad Sháh bahádur.

"Auspicious coin of the noble monarch Muhammad Sháh bahádur."

Reverse. سنة ۲ جلوس میمنت مانوس ضرب جهالوار

Sanah 2. (1 to 21) *julús maimanat mánús zarab Jháláwár.*

"Struck at Jháláwár in the 2nd year of his fortunate reign."

The composition of the coins is said to have been 11 máshas of silver and two rattis of khar or alloy.

Weight. The weight of the rupee is said to have been 11¼ máshas. The specimen in my collection weighs 166 grains. The weight of the smaller pieces was in due proportion, viz., ½, ¼, and ⅛ of the weight of the rupee.

The value of the original old Madan Sháhí rupee was 1 rupee 10 annas "kull-dár," but as years passed on the quality of the silver used at the mint is said to have deteriorated, and in the year 1870 the Political Agent at the Court reported to Government that the value of the rupee was only 15 annas "kull-dár." As, however, he also reported that the weight of the rupee was then 11½ máshas, and that the coins of the State were made of pure silver, his information was probably valueless.

2. The new Madan Sháhí coins (1857 to the present day) have the following inscription (see Plate IX. figs. 2, 3, 4, and 5) in the Persian character:

Obverse. ملکه معظمه وکٹوریه بادشاه انگلستان

Malikah-mu'azzamah Victoria bádsháh Inglistán.

"Her Majesty Victoria Queen of England."

Reverse. سنة ۳ جلوس میمنت مانوس ضرب جهالوار

Sanah 3. (1 to 34) *julús maimanat mánús zarab Jháláwár.*

"Struck at Jháláwár in the third year of her fortunate reign."

Symbols on the reverse. Pánch pakhrí ka jháṛ. Pánch pakhri ki phúlli.

Assay. Said to be the same as of the old coin.

Weight. Of the rupee, which is a smaller and thicker coin than the old one, 175 grains, and of the smaller pieces in exact proportion.

Value. The value fluctuates from 1 to 10 pies per rupee, depending much upon the rate of the hundís or native cheques. Sometimes the value of the rupee of the State is only equal to that of the Imperial rupee, it is never less, and is sometimes as much as 4 per cent. higher than that of the Imperial coin.

COPPER COINAGE

The copper coins are oblong or squarish masses, and are badly stamped. They are known as the "Madan Sháhí paisá" or "Madan Sháhí taká." There have been two distinct issues of copper coins corresponding to the two types of silver pieces. The old coin was issued in 1837 and had the same inscription as the old Madan Sháhí rupee. The issue of it was continued yearly until 1857, the "sanah" being changed each year, as in the case of the silver coins. The new coin, now in circulation (see Plate IX. fig. 6), was first issued in A.D. 1857. Copper coins are minted every year. The coins of the present issue bear the "sanát" 1 to 34, as in the case of the silver coins which correspond with them, "sanah 1" corresponding to the latter part of the year A.D. 1857. The coins bear the same inscription as the new Madan Sháhí rupees, and the same symbols. The average weight of the specimens is about 280 grains.

The value of the copper coins is constantly fluctuating, formerly the rate was 23 takás to a Madan Sháhí rupee, but at the present time (end of A.D. 1891) it is 34 takás to the rupee.

The copper coins of the State are now made from plates of copper obtained from Bombay.

JAISALMER CURRENCIES

JAISALMER

CAPITAL JAISALMER

Jaisalmer has an area of 16,039 square miles. The population in 1891 was 115,701, or 7 persons per square mile. The revenue is stated to be about £10,000 a year, a very small one considering the area, but to be accounted for by the fact that the greater portion of the land belongs to the feudal chiefs related to the ruling family. This tract of country was comprehended, in ancient days, under the term "Marusthali," the desert of India.

The ruling family is of the Yadu race, whose power was paramount in India 3,000 years ago. The Yadus settled in the desert in the 8th century, where Tunnote was the first seat of their power. Lodorva, an ancient city 10 miles north-west of the present city of Jaisalmer, was for many years the capital of the dynasty, but, soon after the foundations of Jaisalmer were laid (A.D. 1156), it was abandoned.

Subbul Singh was the first of the princes of Jaisalmer who held his dominions as a fief of the Muhammadan Empire.

In December, 1818, a treaty of perpetual friendship, alliance, and unity of interests was concluded between the East India Company and the Maháráwul Múl Ráj. The date shows that this State was one of the last to be received under the protection of the British Government.

LIST OF THE JAISALMER CHIEFS FROM 1722

Name	Date of ascending the Gaddi	Date of death
1. Akhey Singh (Akhaya Siṇha)	A.D. 1722	A.D. 1762
2. Múl Ráj	,, 1762	,, 1819
3. Gaj Singh	,, 1819	,, 1846
4. Ranjít Singh	,, 1846	,, 1864
5. Benial Singh	,, 1864	Now living.

THE MINT

The mint was established in the year A.D. 1756 by Máháráwul Akhey Singh. Before the issue of the local currency the Muhammad Sháhi coins were the circulating medium.

Múl Ráj, who succeeded Akhey Singh, obtained a farmán from the Imperial Court sanctioning the coinage, which up to that time had been issued in defiance of orders from Dehlí.

The Akhey Sháhí coins were originally very pure. They contained only 2½ per cent. of alloy, but the issue gradually deteriorated until the alloy reached as much as 12 per cent.

The original weight of the Akhey Sháhí rupee was 168.75 grains, or 10½ máshas of the old Jaisalmer tola, each másha being equal to 16 grains. The coin consisted of 164.53 grains of silver and 4.22 grains of alloy. When the amount of alloy was increased the weight of the coin remained nominally at the old standard. Thakúr Kesrí Singh, who for some years managed the Jaisalmer affairs, tried to restore the purity of the currency by lessening the alloy, but as he at the same time reduced the weight of the coin he found it was distrusted, and he was obliged to abandon the issue of the light coins. His rupee weighed 162½ grains, being composed of 158½ grains of silver and four grains of alloy.

The coins have always been known as the "Akhey Sháhí" from their first issue to the present day. They were formerly current throughout Sind, Bhawulpur, Mullaní, Jhalore, and the Jaisalmer territory; they are now almost restricted to the latter.

GOLD COINAGE

No gold coins were issued before the year A.D. 1860. The gold coins now in use are the muhr, half-muhr, quarter-muhr, and one-eighth of a muhr. See Plate IX. fig. 8, but in gold, for the inscription, and figs. 9, 10, 11, and 12, for the sizes of average coins.

Inscription as in silver coins No. 2.

Assay. The pieces are said to be of pure gold.

Weight. Of the muhr 167 grains, and of the smaller pieces in proportion.

SILVER COINAGE

1. Coins struck in the name of Muhammad Sháh; the pieces are the rupee, eight-anna, and four-anna. See Plate IX. fig. 7.

INSCRIPTION.

Obverse. سکه مبارک صاحب قران ثاني محمد شاه بادشاه غازي ۱۱۵۲

Sikka mubárak sáhib kirán sány Muhammad Sháh bádshâh ghází 1152.

"Auspicious coin of the 2nd sáhib kirán (lord of the fortunate conjunction of planets) the victorious Emperor Muhammad Sháh, A.H. 1152."

Symbols. Circles of dots, the Hindí numerals in the *n* of *kirán* on some of the coins.

Reverse. سنة ۲۲ جلوس ميمنت مانوس

Sanah 22 julús maimanat mánús.

"In the 22nd year of his fortunate reign."

The year 22 was copied from the Dehlí Muhammad Sháhí rupee, which was taken as the model for the original Akhey Sháhí coin.

Symbols. Circles of dots, these marks  of the mint-master under the word *sanah*.

2. Coins struck in the Queen's name. See Plate IX. fig. 8, and figs. 16, 13, and 14, for the sizes of the smaller pieces.

The coins of this issue are the rupee, eight-anna, four-anna, and two-anna bits. They were introduced in the year 1860 (S. 1917), but were not brought into circulation until the year 1863. They are also called Akhey Sháhí.

INSCRIPTION.

Obverse. سکه مبارک انگلستان وکتوریا فرمان رواي ملکه معظمه
رفيع الدرجه

Sikka mubárak Inglistán Victoria farmán rawái malikah mu'azzamah rafí'ud-darajah

"Auspicious coins of Victoria lawful Queen of England, Her Majesty's ally"

Symbols. Circles of dots.

Reverse. سنة ۲۲ جلوس میمنت مانوس ضرب دار الریاست جیسلمیر

Sanah 22 julús maimanat mánus zarab dár-al-riyásat Jaisalmer.

"Struck (coin) in the house of Government Jaisalmer in the 22nd year of her fortunate reign" (should be the 24th year, the numerals 22 were probably continued from an earlier coin).

Symbols. Circles of dots, the Pálam (sacred bird), which was introduced for luck, as in former times the Pálam gave a very auspicious omen to the Jaisalmer people; and the chhátá or royal umbrella.

Weight. Of the rupee 162¼ grains, and of the smaller coins in proportion.

Value. Of the rupee 15 annas Imperial.

COPPER COINAGE

The only copper coin ever made in this State was the "Dodia," which is still in circulation. It was first struck in Samvat 1716 (A.D. 1660), and a further issue was made in Samvat 1893. The Ráj officials say that these coins were only made during these two years. The coins bear a pattern on both surfaces, the marks appear to me to be not unlike those on the Mewár paisa (Dhingla), see page 13 and Plate II. fig. 8. The marks on the coins are said, by the Ráj officials, to be without signification. See Plate IX. fig. 15.

Value. Forty of these small pieces go to an anna, they are used instead of kaurís (cowries).

Weight. About 18 to 20 grains.

ALWAR CURRENCIES

ONE RUPEE
ALWAR STATE
ONE RUPEE
ALWAR STATE

ALWAR

CAPITAL ALWAR

This State has an area of 3051 square miles. It is bounded on the north by the British District of Gurgáon, the Báwal pargana of Nábhá State, and the Koṭ Kásim pargana of Jaipur; on the east by the Bhartpur State and Gurgáon district; on the south and west by the State of Jaipur. The revenue is about £232,000 a year. In 1891 the population was 767,786, or 252 persons per square mile.

Originally the State consisted of a number of petty Chiefships, which, till the middle of the last century, owed allegiance to Jaipur and Bhartpur. The founder of the Mahárájá's family was Pratáp Singh, a Narúka Rajpút, who at first possessed but two villages and a half, Machári being one of them. During the minority of the Mahárájá of Jaipur, and while Játs, Mughals, and Maráthás were contending with each other, he succeeded, between A.D. 1771 and 1776, in establishing independent power in the greater part of the territory which forms the southern portion of the present State. In the war carried on by Mírza Majíf Khán against the Játs, he united his forces at an opportune moment with those of the former, and aided him in defeating the enemy at Barsána and at Díg. As a reward for his services he obtained the title of Ráo Rájá, and a sanad authorizing him to hold Machári direct. In 1776 he took advantage of the weakness of Bhartpur, to wrest from the Játs the town and fort of Alwar. His brethren of the Narúka clan then acknowleged him as their Chief. At the commencement of the Maráthá war of 1803–6, Bakhtáwar Singh allied himself with the British Government. After the campaign, the British Government conferred on him the northern part of the present State. In 1803 the Chief accepted the protection of the British Government, and a treaty of alliance was concluded, on the basis that Alwar should pay no tribute, but that the troops of the State should be at the service of the Government when required.

The Chief had the title of Ráo-Rájá, but at the jubilee of the Queen-Empress the title of Mahárájá was conferred on the present ruler.

LIST OF THE CHIEFS FROM FOUNDATION OF GADDI TO DATE

Name	Date of birth	Date of accession	Date of death
1. Pratáp Singh (Son of Rao Mahabhat Singh)	A.D. 1741	1772[1]	1791
2. Bakhtáwar Singh (An adopted son)	A.D. 1776	1791	1815
3. Bani Singh (Nephew and adopted son)	A.D. 1809	1815	1857
4. Sheodan Singh (Son of Bani Singh)	A.D. 1846	1857	1874
5. Mangal Singh, G.C.S.I. (Selected from the Thánna family, there being no direct heir.)	A.D. ——	1874	Now living

THE MINT

Only one mint was worked in this State. The mint was located at Rájgarh. It was opened in the year 1772. Silver coins were issued every year until 1876, when an arrangement was made for the rupee of the State to be struck at the Calcutta mint, the Mahárájá being willing, in the interests of his people, to forego the honour and glory of using the coins wrought at his own mint. Since the year 1877, when the first coins were made for the State at the Calcutta mint, a few rupees have been made once a year at the Rájgarh mint as a matter of form, these are kept in the Tosha khána at Alwar, and are not circulated.

Gold has never been coined in the State. Before the year 1877 the coins were called the "Ráo Sáhí," both nazr and ordinary rupees were regularly coined.

SILVER COINAGE

Before the year 1877, the coins of the State were the rupee, eight-anna, and four-anna bits, since that date no coin of less value than the rupee has been made. The last eight-anna and four-anna pieces were, how-

[1] Year of building the Rájgarh Fort.

ever, struck in the year 1852. (For sizes of the eight-anna and four-anna bits, see Plate X. figs. 2 and 8.)

1. Coins of Ráo Rájá Pratáp Singh. See Plate X. fig. 1.

INSCRIPTION.

Obverse. سکه مبارک بادشاه غازي شاه عالم

Sikka Mubárak bádsháh ghází Sháh 'Álam.

"Auspicious coin of the victorious Emperor Sháh 'Álam."

Reverse. ضرب راجگره سنة جلوس ميمنت مانوس

Zarab Rájgarh sanah julús maimanat mánús.

"Struck at Rájgarh in the second year of his fortunate reign."

Symbols. Dots to fill in the intervals.

Weight. This is put down as 173–5 grains, and the pure contents at 167.23 grains by the Calcutta Assay Tables. The intrinsic value of 100 rupees was stated to be 101.353 Imperial rupees. The rupees I have seen weigh about 171¼ grains.

2. Pratáp Singh's second issue. See Plate X. fig. 3.

The pieces are the rupee, eight-anna and four-anna bits.

Inscription, the same as on the former coin. My specimen bears date *sanah* 19 (A.D. 1791).

Symbols. Obverse.  over the *h* of *bádsháh*.

Reverse. A jháṛ above the word *sanah*, the tip of the jháṛ directed downwards. Dots to fill in the spaces.

Weight. This is said by the Calcutta mint authorities to be the same as in No. 1, but I have not met with a specimen above 171¼ grains in weight.

The above-mentioned coins were also used during the reign of Bakhtáwar Singh.

3. Bani Singh's coins. See Plate X. fig. 5.

INSCRIPTION.

Obverse. سکه مبارک بادشاه غازي محمد بهادر شاه ۱۲۶۱

Sikka mubárak bádsháh ghází Muhammad Bahádur Sháh, 1261.

"Auspicious coin of the victorious Emperor Muhammad Bahádur Sháh, A.H. 1261."

Symbols. under the *sháh* of *bádsháh*; by the word *mubárak*; over the *h* of *bádsháh.*

Reverse. The same inscription as in No. 1.

Symbols. A jháṛ placed horizontally over the word *sanah*, and dots.

Weight. 174 grains.

This coin was in circulation during the first two years of the reign of Sheodan Singh.

4. Sheodan Singh's coins. See Plate X. fig. 10. These were introduced in the year 1859, and coined up to the year 1874.

Inscription.

Obverse. ملکه معظمه تخت نشین دارال سلطنت انگلستان
سکه مبارک سنة عیسوي ۱۸۶۷

Malikah mu'azzamah takht nashín dár-al-saltanat Inglistán sikkah mubárak sanah 'Iswy, 1867.

"Auspicious coin of Her Majesty the Queen, England the seat of Empire, in the year of Jesus 1867."

Symbols. The chhátá, or royal umbrella; a jháṛ with three points on one side; a small jhár under the word *mu'azzamah*; a circle of dots over the word *mubárak*; a small jháṛ over *Inglistán.*

Reverse. ضرب راجگه مهاراجادیراج مهاراو راج سري سواي
شیودان سنگه بهادر سنة ۱۰ جلوس

Zarab Rájgarh Mahárájádhiráj Mahárao ráj sri sawái Sheodan Singh bahádur sanah 10 *julús.*

"Struck at Rájgarh in the 10th year of the reign of the great king Máharao-ráj Sheodan Singh."

Symbols. The chhátá, the jháṛ, and a small second jháṛ over the word *sawái*, also a badly formed jháṛ at the lower part of the coin.[1]

Weight. 174 grains.

5. H.H. the Mahárájá Mangal Singh's coins, A.D. 1874–1876. See Plate X. fig. 12.

Inscription.

Obverse. The same inscription as on No. 4, but with the date altered.

[1] For the unusual arrangement of the inscription (in two directions on each surface) see the figure.

Symbols. No chhátá, no jháŗ over the word *mu'azzamah*, a circle of dots over *mubárak*, a badly executed jháŗ under *Inglistán*.

Reverse. مهاراو راج سواي منگل سنگه بهادر ضرب راجگه سنة جلوس ۱

Mahárúo-ráj sawái Mangal Singh baháдar zarab Rájgarh sanah julús I.

"Struck at Rájgarh in the first year of the reign of Mahárúo-ráj Mangal Singh."

Symbols. A jháŗ placed transversely, a one-sided jháŗ by the side of the word *julús*.

Weight. 174 grains.

6. Mangal Singh's coin, 1877 to the year 1888. See Plate X. fig. 11. These coins are milled and are made at the Calcutta mint.

INSCRIPTION.

Obverse. "Victoria Empress," in English. The Queen's head.

Reverse—in the centre. مهاراو راج سواي منگل سنگه بهادر ۱۸۸۰

Mahárúo-ráj sawái Mangal Singh bahádur, 1880.

In the border "One rupee," and "Alwar State" in English. Two jháŗs, each of 15 branches.

Weight. 180 grains.

7. Coin of Mangal Singh, 1888 to the present day. See Plate X. fig. 13.

INSCRIPTION.

Obverse the same as in No. 6.

Reverse—in the centre. مهاراج سري سواي منگل سنگه بهادر ۱۸۹۱

Mahárúj srí sawái Mangal Singh bahádur, 1891.

(The Mahárájá's Title.)

The border as in No. 6.

Weight. 180 grains.

Assay and value of the coins. The Rájgarh rupee weighed 11 máshas. The original coin contained 10 máshas 5½ rattis of silver, and 2½ rattis of copper. In A.D. 1860 (S. 1917) Capt. Impey, the Political Agent, altered the composition to 10 máshas 3½ rattis of silver, and 4½ rattis of copper.

In 1864 (S. 1921) the Chief again changed the composition, and issued coin composed of 10 máshas 2 rattis of silver, and 6 rattis of copper. In 1866 (S. 1923) the Chief altered the coin back to the original standard.

A hundred original Rájgarh rupees contained 97.2 by weight of silver, and 2.14 by weight of copper. The Imperial rupee contains 91.3 by weight of silver, and 8.13 by weight of copper. According to Prinsep's *Useful Tables*[1] the weight of the rupee was 173.75 grains; the pure contents were put down as 167.23 grains; the assay as Br. 11; the touch as 96.2. The value of 100 rupees in Imperial money was, in Prinsep's time, 101.353. The additional exchange rate of the Rájgarh coin is said to have varied at different times from 1 to 7 rupees Imperial.

The assay and weight of the Alwar coins made at Calcutta is the same as that of the Imperial coins.

COPPER COINAGE

The copper coin of the State is known as the "Ráo Sáhí Taká."

1. Pratáp Singh's coin. See Plate X. fig. 4.

INSCRIPTION.

Obverse. محمد عالم شاه بادشاه غازي

Muhammad 'Alam Sháh bádsháh ghází.

"The victorious Emperor Muhammad 'Alam Sháh."

Reverse. As in the silver pieces No. 1.

Weight. 281 grains.

2. Bakhtáwar Singh's coin, A.D. 1791–1815. See Plate X. fig. 6.

Obverse. As in No. 1, with the addition of the words *sikka mubárak.*

Reverse. The same as in No. 1.

Weight. 290 grains.

3. Bani Singh's coin, 1815–1857. See Plate X. fig. 7.

Obverse. محمد بهادر شاه بادشاه غازي

Muhammad bahádur Sháh bádsháh ghází.

"The victorious Emperor Muhammad Sháh bahádur."

Reverse. As in No. 1.

Weight. 281 grains.

[1] Page 58.

4. Sheodan Singh's coin, 1859–1874. See Plate X. fig. 9.

Obverse. سکه مبارک ملکه معظمه تخت نشین دارال سلطنت انگلستان

Sikka mubárak malikah mu'azzamah takht nashín dár al saltanat Inglistán.

"Auspicious coin of Her Majesty the Queen, England the seat of Empire."

Reverse. مہاراج ادیراج مہاراو راج ساوي شیودان سنگه ضرب راجگره

Mahárájá-dhiráj Mahárdo ráj sawái Sheodán Singh zarab Rájgarh.

"Struck at Rájgarh by the great king Mahárão ráj sawái Sheodan Singh."

Symbols. over the word *saltanat* on the obverse; under *zarab* on the reverse.

Weight. 285 grains.

5. Mangal Singh's coin, struck as a matter of form each year, but not brought into circulation. 1874 to date.

Obverse and reverse the same as the silver coins No. 5.

Since the year 1873 the British quarter-anna copper coin has been the copper circulating medium. A large quantity of this coin was imported for the purpose. Since 1873 the Ráo Sáhí coins have not been issued. On the 30th of December, 1879, the Durbar sent a request, through the Political Agent, that the Government of India would issue a special Alwar copper coin on the same terms, as regards device and currency, throughout India, as it did in the case of the Alwar rupee. This request was refused, as the Government is anxious gradually to do away with the local coins.

Value of the Ráo Sáhí coins. The value in Imperial coin has been the subject of great variation, as it fluctuated according to the relative value of the Imperial and Hálí Alwar rupee (rupee of the current year). The exchange rate of the copper coin for the Ráo Sáhí rupee varied from 16 to 28, the rate for the Imperial rupee being 2 or 3 paise less. When Impey wrote his letter to Government about the Alwar coinage, he stated that "36" paisá went to the rupee; I am informed that this statement must have been incorrect.

KARAULI

PLATE XI

1

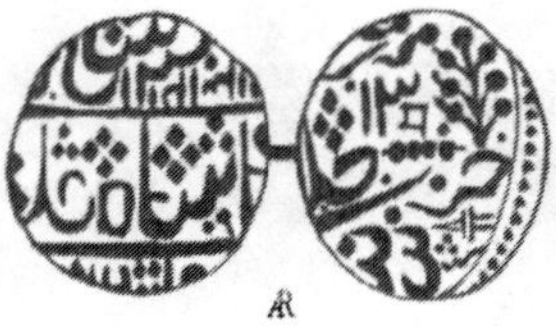

AR

2

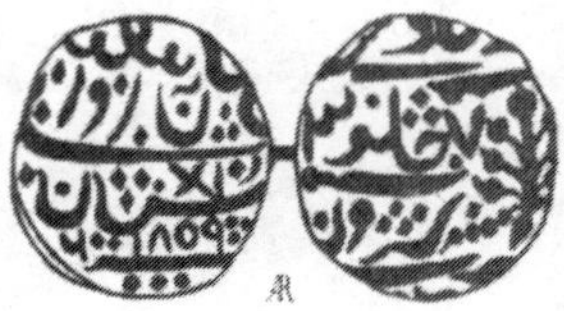

AR

3

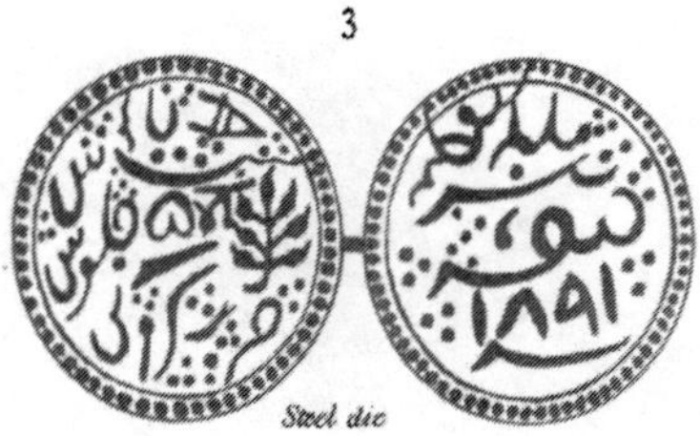

Steel die

4

AR

5

AR

6

AR

7

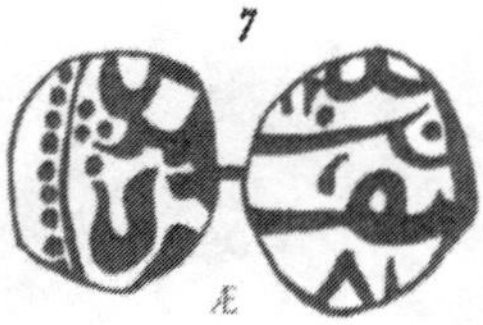

Æ

8

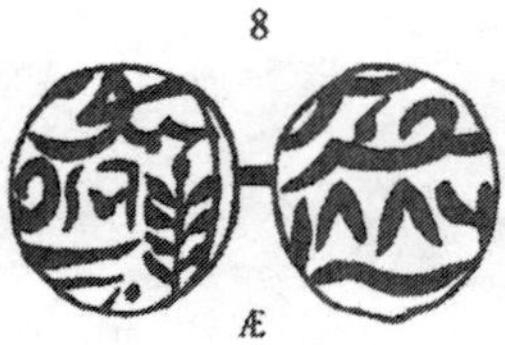

Æ

KARAULI

CAPITAL KARAULI

The area of Karauli is 1,229 square miles; in 1891 the population was 156,587 or 127 persons per square mile; the rent-roll is over £48,000 a year.

The Mahárájá of Karauli is the head of the Jádun clan of Rájputs, who claim descent from Krishna. The clan has always remained in or near the country of Braj, round Muttra.

LIST OF THE CHIEFS FROM A.D. 1724 TO THE PRESENT DAY

Name	Father's name	Date of succession	Date of Death
1. Gopál Singh	Kawur Pál	A.D. 1724	1757, S. 1814
2. Tursum Pál	Son Pál	A.D. 1757	1772, S. 1829
3. Manak Pál	Tursum Pál	A.D. 1772	1804, S. 1861
4. Harbaksh Pál	Manak Pál	A.D. 1804	1838, S. 1894
5. Pratáp Pál	Ráo Amar Pál	A.D. 1838	1848, S. 1905
6. Nar Singh Pál	Sheo Pál	A.D. 1848	1853, S. 1909
7. Madan Pál	Gordhun Pál	A.D. 1853	1869, S. 1926
8. Jai Singh Pál	Narayan Pál	A.D. 1869	1875, S. 1932
9. Arjan Pál	Mangal Pál	A.D. 1875	1886, S. 1943
10. Bhanwar Pál	Durjan Pál	A.D. 1886	Now living.

THE MINT

In the year A.D. 1870 the Political Agent reported to Government that the mint was started about 100 years ago by Mahárájá Gopál Singh. I feel sure that this statement is incorrect; I have been unable to find any coins of the State older than Sháh 'Alam's time. The first coins in this State were doubtless those struck by Mahárájá Manak Pál about the year 1780.

Gold has not been coined, but both silver and copper are issued. The mint is located at the capital.

The distinctive mint-marks of this State are the "jháṛ" and the "kaṭár" (dagger). From the time of Mahárájá Madan Pál to the present day each Chief has placed his initial letter on his silver coins. म stands for Madan Pál; ज for Jai Singh Pãl; अ for Arjan Pál; and भ for the name of the present Chief, Mahárájá Bhanwar Pál. The "sanah julús" reckons the years from the date of succession of the Chiefs. The mint dároga puts a mark on the coins, and available spaces are filled with dots as in the coins of other States.

In 1870, the Political Agent reported that the coin (rupee) weighed 11 máshas and 2 rattis, of which 10 máshas 6½ rattis were silver, and 3½ rattis were copper. The coins now being issued are of the same composition. At the present time I am informed by the Durbar authorities, through Capt. Herbert, the Political Agent, that the value of the rupee is sometimes equal to that of the Imperial coin, and sometimes as much as 12 annas per cent. less; the value is continually fluctuating. In 1870 the Political Agent stated that the value of the rupee was 16½ annas Imperial.

The silver coins at present issued are the rupee, eight-anna, and four-anna pieces; the smaller pieces are not often coined, or in any great quantities.

Karauli is written in Persian with either ق or ک.

SILVER COINAGE

1. Coin struck in the name of Sháh 'Álam by Mahárájá Manak Pál (A.D. 1772–1804). See Plate XI. fig. 1.

Obverse. سکه مبارک شاه عالم غازي صاحب قران ثاني سنة هجري

Sikka mubárak Sháh 'Álam ghází sáhib kirán sány sanah Hijrí, and some Persian numerals.

"Auspicious coin of the victorious Emperor Sháh 'Álam, the second *sáhib kirán* (lord of the fortunate conjunction of planets), the Hijrí year."

Reverse. ضرب قرولي سنه جلوس ميمنت مانوس

Zarab Karauli sanah julús maimanat mánús.

"Struck at Karauli in the year of his fortunate reign."

On the reverses of some of the coins of this issue the word *Ráj* is said to precede *Karauli*.

Symbols. Crosses made by dots over the *sh* and *h* of *sháh*, and the *j* of *julús*; on the reverse the jháṛ and kaṭár, and this mark ◆ between the word sanah and the numerals 13.

Weight. 170 grains. In Prinsep's *Useful Tables*,[1] these coins are described as weighing 171.37 grains, and as having 163.16 grains pure contents. The intrinsic value of 100 coins is stated at 98.877 kull-dár rupees.

2. Coin issued by Mahárájá Madan Pál, on the authority of a kharíta received from Sir George Lawrence, agent to the Governor-General, dated 28th of August, 1858. On some of the coins of this issue sanah "1852" appears; this is an error, the sanah should be "1859." The mistake was seen at the time of issue, and arose through the similarity between the Persian numerals "2" and "9." Madan Pál did not succeed to the gaddí until 1853. The coins of this issue were the rupee and half-rupee. See Plate XI. fig. 2.

INSCRIPTION.

Obverse. As in reverse of No. 1. "Struck at Karauli in the year of the fortunate reign."

Symbols. The jháṛ, kaṭár, a sword, and the letter म, being the initial of the Chief's name.

Reverse. ملكه معظمه فرمان رواي انگلستان سنه ۱۸۵۹

Malikah mu'azzamah farmán rawái Inglistán sanah 1859.

"Of the Empress, lawful Queen of England, A.D. 1859."

Symbols. The Hindí numeral 6, dotsunder sanah, this mark X over *Inglistán*.

Weight. 170 grains.

3. Coin struck by Arjan Pál and by the present Chief, Bhanwar Pál. See Plate XI. fig. 3, which is from the die at the mint, and figs. 4, 5, and 6, for sizes of average coins.

INSCRIPTION.

Obverse. As in reverse of No. 1. "Struck at Karauli in the year of the fortunate reign."

Symbols. The jháṛ, dagger, and the initial letter भ or अ.

[1] p. 56.

Reverse. ملكه معظمه قيصر هند سنة ١٨٩١

Malikah mu'azzamah kaisar-i-Hind sanah 1891.

"Of Her Majesty the Empress of India, in the year 1891."

Symbols. Dots.

Weight. 170 grains.

COPPER COINAGE

1. Coin issued by Manak Pál.

Inscription. The same as on silver coin No. 1.

Weight. When Prinsep wrote he mentioned that the Karauli copper coin weighed 281 grains, that 36 went to the rupee, and that they were current in Dehlí and Karauli.[1]

2. Coin corresponding to the silver issue No. 2, and with the same inscription. In 1870 the Political Agent wrote to Government that these paisá weighed 18 máshas, and that ordinarily 44 went to the rupee.

3. Paisá now being issued. See Plate XI. figs. 7 and 8. It bears the same inscription and symbols as the silver coins No. 3. At the present time 68 paisá, or 34 "takás" are equal to one rupee. Sometimes the value of the local paisá is equal to the British paisá in value, but as a rule it is less in value, as 64 British paisá or 32 "takás" go to the rupee. The weight of the present Karauli paisá is 280 grains.

STATEMENT SHEWING THE AMOUNTS OF SILVER AND COPPER ISSUED FROM THE KARAULI MINT FROM SAMVAT 1942 TO SAMVAT 1947 (A.D. 1885–1890)

Year	Weight of silver	Weight of copper
Samvat 1942	24¾ seers	1512 maunds, 8 seers
„ 1943	1 maund, 1 seer	1273 „ 25 „
„ 1944	15 maunds, 22½ seers	135 „ 23 „
„ 1945	13 „ 4 „	Nil
„ 1946	18 „ 25¾ „	„
„ 1947	9 „ 30¾ „	„

[1] *Useful Tables*, p. 63.

BHARTPUR CURRENCIES

BHARTPUR

I
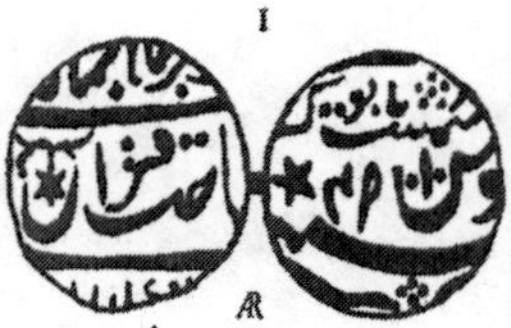
AR

2

Steel die

3
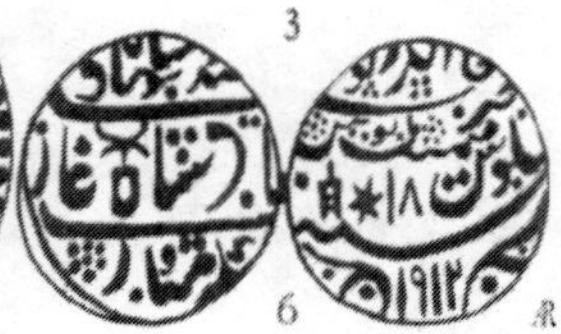
AR

4
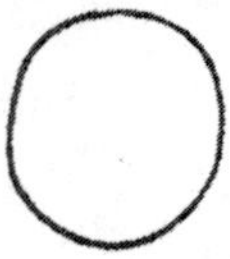
AR

5

AR

6
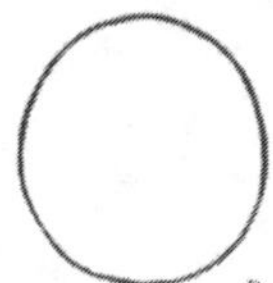
AR

7
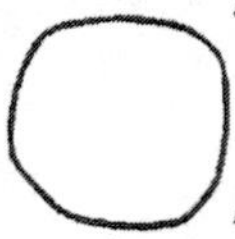
Æ

8

AR

9

Steel die

10
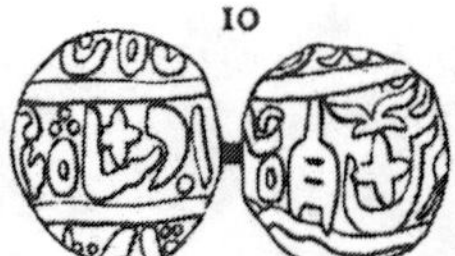
AR

9

Steel die

DHOLPUR

10

AR

11

Steel die

12

AR

BHARTPUR

CAPITAL BHARTPUR

Area, 1,961 square miles. Population (in 1891), 640,303, or 327 persons per square mile. Revenue about £280,000 a year.

The Bhartpur is a Jhát family; it was founded by Churaman, who abandoned the plough to lead his countrymen against their tyrants, the Muhammadans. The Játs were from early times noted freebooters; they are mentioned in Ferishtá as molesting Mahmúd of Ghazní, on his return from Gujarát in A.D. 1026. During the prosperity of the Mughal Empire the turbulence of their character brought upon them more than once the Imperial wrath. It was during the anarchy which followed on the death of Aurangzeb that the foundation of the Bhartpur kingdom was laid; Badan Singh, who dispossessed his brother Churaman, was proclaimed at Díg as leader of the Játs, with the title of Takhur. Ranjít Singh of Bhartpur was one of the first Chiefs of Northern India to connect his interests with those of the British Government.

LIST OF THE BHARTPUR CHIEFS FROM A.D. 1723 TO 1892

Name	Father's name	Year of succession	Year of death
1. Badan Singh	Bhao Singh	1723	1756
2. Súraj Mal	Badan Singh	1756	1763
3. Jawahir Singh	Súraj Mal	1763	1768
4. Ratan Singh	Súraj Mal	1768	1769
5. Kehrí Singh	Súraj Mal	1769	1777
6. Ranjít Singh	Súraj Mal	1777	1805
7. Randhir Singh	Ranjít Singh	1805	1823
8. Baldeo Singh	Ranjít Singh	1823	1825
9. Durjan Sal[1]	Lachman Singh	1825	1826
10. Balwant Singh	Baldeo Singh	1826	1852
11. Jaswant Singh	Balwant Singh	1852	Now reigning

[1] Usurped the gaddi for nine months after the death of Baldeo Singh, but was deposed by the British Government.

THE MINT

At first there were two mints in the State—at Díg and Bhartpur-town, they are said to have been opened by Súraj Mal in Samvat 1820 (A.D. 1763). For many years the Bhartpur mint has alone been worked.

In 1870 the Political Agent reported to Government that there was only one mint in the State—that at the Capital, where rupees were made; that the rupee was eleven máshas in weight, and was of about the same value as the kull-dár coin. The officials of the State now inform me through Lieut.-Colonel Martelli, the Political Agent, that the Díg mint was re-opened, and that coins were issued from it up to S. 1935 (A.D. 1878), when it was finally closed.

The Bhartpur másha is equal to 8 rattis; a ratti to 2¼ grains.

No silver coins have been struck in the State during the last six years.

Symbols have been placed on the coins at the pleasure of the Chiefs, and by these the specimens are distinguished. The most usual are the "dagger" (*kaṭár*), the "stick" (*laṭh*), and the "flower" (*phúlli*).

SILVER COINAGE

1. The Díg rupee struck in the name of Sháh 'Álam, and having the same inscription as the Bhartpur rupee No. 1. It was issued in or about A.D. 1763.

2. The Díg coins issued in the name of Akbar II. These coins are said to have been first made in the time of Mahárájá Randhir Singh. The coins of the issue were the rupee, half-rupee, and quarter-rupee. See Plate XII. fig. 1.

INSCRIPTION.

Obverse. سكه مبارک صاحب قران ثاني محمد اكبر شاه

Sikka mubárak sáhib kirán sány Muhammad Akbar Sháh.

"Auspicious coin of the 2nd *sáhib kirán* (lord of the fortunate conjunction of planets), Muhammad Akbar the King."

Symbols. A star above the *n* of *kirán*.

Reverse. ۴۲ or ۴۹ ضرب مندرپور سنة جلوس میمنت مانوس

Zarab Mahunderpur sanah julús maimanat mánús. Sanah 42 or 49? on my specimen.

"Struck at Mahunderpur in the 42nd year of his fortunate reign."

Symbols. A star after the *sanah* 42? this figure •|• in the curl of the *s* of *julús*.

Weight. 172 grains. Assay. The same as the present Bhartpur rupee. Prinsep gives the weight of the Díg rupee at 169.70 grains, the pure contents at 150.25 grains, the value of 100 coins at 91.064 kull-dár coins.[1]

3. Rupee struck at Bhartpur in the name of Sháh 'Álam, and said to have been issued in A.D. 1763 by Mahárájá Súraj Mal. See Plate XII. fig. 10.

INSCRIPTION.

Obverse. سکه مبارک بادشاه غازي شاه عالم

Sikka mubárak bádsháh ghází Sháh 'Alam.

"Auspicious coin of the victorious Emperor Sháh 'Álam."

Symbols. A cross over the *sh* of *bádshah*.

Reverse. ضرب برج انورپور سنة جلوس

Zarab burji anwarpur sanah julús.

"Struck at the city of the tower of glory."

Symbols. The dagger, a cross in the curl of the *s* of *julús*, and a flower over it.

Weight. 171.86 grains.

4. Bhartpur coins struck in the name of Akbar II. (1806–1837). See Plate XII. fig. 3. These coins are said to have been issued by Randhir Singh.

INSCRIPTION.

Obverse. سکه مبارک صاحب قران ثاني محمد اکبرشاه بادشاه غازي

Sikka mubárak sáhib kirán sány Muhammad Akbar Sháh bádshdh ghází.

"Auspicious coin of the 2nd sáhib kirán, the noble monarch Muhammad Akbar Sháh."

[1] *Useful Tables*, p. 54.

Symbols. A circle of dots after the word *mubárak*, a flower over the *h* of *bádsháh*.

Reverse. سنة ۱۸ جلوس میمنت مانوس ضرب برج انورپور ضرب ۱۹۱۲

Sánah 18 *julús maimanat mánús zarab burji anwurpur zarab* 1912.

"Struck at the city of the tower of glory in S. 1912, in the 18th year of his fortunate reign."

Symbols. The dagger, a star after the *sanah*, circles of dots.

Weight. 171.86 grains. Pure contents, 164.70 grains. The value of 100 rupees is equal to 99.819 rupees kull-dár.[1]

5. Coins struck in the year A.D. 1858. See Plate XII. fig. 2, which is from the die at the mint, and for the sizes of ordinary coins, see figs. 6, 4, 5, and 8.

INSCRIPTION.

Obverse. ضرب بهرتپور برج انور سواي جسونت سنگه بهادر جنگ ۱۹۱۰

Zarab Bhartpur Burji-anwar sawái Jaswant Singh bahádur jung 1910.

"Struck at Bhartpur, the town of glory, in 1910, by his Excellency Jaswant Singh Bahádur, the champion."

Symbols. The dagger and a star in the same line as the date, this sign  after the word *singh*.

Reverse. جناب ملکه معظمه کوین وکتوریه فرمان رواي انگلند سنة ۱۸۵۸

Janáb malikah mu'azzamah Queen Victoria farmán rawái Ingland sanah 1858. The Queen's head to the right.

"In the year 1858 of her Majesty Queen Victoria lawful sovereign of England."

Weight. About 171-2 grains. The rupee is said by the officials of the State to contain 4 rattis of copper alloy less than the Imperial coin, and to be 4 rattis less in weight.

The coins of this issue are the rupee, eight-anna, four-anna, and two-anna pieces.

COPPER COINAGE

Only one type of copper coin has been issued in this State from the foundation of the mint to the present day. The coin is said to

[1] Prinsep *op. cit.* p 53.

have been first issued by Mahárájá Súraj Mal about the year 1763. Of course many dies have been in use, and slight variations are in consequence found in the arrangement of the inscription on the coins. See Plate XII. fig. 9, and for the size of an average coin see fig. 7.

Inscription. The same as on the silver coin No. 1.

Symbols. The dagger on all the coins which I have seen, in addition on some a flower above the *s* of *julús*, on others a star above the shoulder of the dagger, and the "laṭh" above the *s* of *julús*.

Weight. The specimens I have met with weigh about 280–4 grains, but I am told by the officials that the proper weight is 18 máshas, or three times the weight of the Imperial paisá (quarter-anna). Prinsep put down the weight at 275 grains.[1]

Value. This depends on the price of copper in the market, and is continually fluctuating.

TABLE SHOWING THE AMOUNT OF COPPER COINED IN THE STATE FROM A.D. 1884 TO 1891

Samvat 1941	784,254 Takás
,, 1942	3,925,178 ,,
,, 1943	1,000,732 ,,
,, 1944	27,736 ,,

No copper coins were issued from S. 1944 to S. 1948.

[1] *Useful Tables*, p. 62.

DHOLPUR CURRENCIES

DHOLPUR

CAPITAL DHOLPUR

This State has an area of 1156 square miles. In 1891 it had a population of about 279,890, or 242 persons per square mile; the revenue is stated to be over £71,000 a year.

The reigning family is a Ját, one of the Bamráolia clan, belonging to the Deswáli tribe. They joined the Rájputs against the Muhammadans, and received a grant of the territory of Gohad. In 1806, the East India Company made over Dholpur to Maháráná Kírat Singh in exchange for his territory of Gohad, which was given up to Sindhiá. Kírat Singh was succeeded by Bhagwant Singh, who in turn was followed by the present Mahárájá, "Maháráj Ráná Nihal Singh," who was born in 1863, and succeeded to the gaddí on Feb. 9th, 1873.

THE MINT

Silver only has been coined in this State. The mint is located at the capital, and was opened in Samvat 1860 (A.D. 1804), when the State of Gohad was ceded a second time to Ráná Kírat Singh. The coins are known by the name "Tamanchá," signifying "pistol," which is the mark of the State. The coins issued are the rupee and the eight-anna piece, but very few of the latter have ever been struck, and they are rarely seen in circulation.

In 1870, the Political Agent reported that the Tamanchá Sáhí contained less than $\frac{1}{36}$ part of alloy, that the rupee weighed $11\frac{1}{4}$ máshas, was of about the same value as the kull-dár rupee, and was current in Dholpur, Gwalior, and Patíala.

1. Tamanchá coins of A.D. 1804 and subsequent years. See Plate XII. fig. 11, which is taken from the die of the coins at the mint, and does not represent the size of the circulating coins, the latter bearing only a portion of the inscription, as is the case with the more modern coins of the State. See figs. 10 and 12.

INSCRIPTION.

Obverse. سکه زد بر هفت کشور سایه فضل الله حامي دين محمد
شاه عالم بادشاه سنة ١٢١٨

Sikka zad bar haft kishwar sáyah fazl Allah hámi din Muhammad Sháh 'Álam bádshúh sanah 1218.

"By the grace of God, the defender of the faith Muhammad Sháh 'Álam, the king, in the year A.H. 1218 (A.D. 1803–4) struck coin in the seven climes."

Symbols. The pistol in the middle of the coin.

Reverse. ضرب گوهد سنة جلوس ٤٦ ميمنت مانوس
Zarab Gohad sanah julús 46 *maimanat mánús.*

"Struck at Gohad in the 46th year of his fortunate reign."

Symbols. This mark  over the word *julús.*

2. Coins of Kírat Singh struck in the name of Akbar II. When in Sanah H. 1221 (A.D. 1806) Akbar II. succeeded at Dehlí, Kírat Singh issued coins in his name with the same inscription as Tamanchá Sáhí No. 4, but bearing A.H. 1221 and the words *Zarab Dholpur* instead of *Zarab Gohad.* This issue was no doubt continued until A.H. 1225. The coins have the Tamanchá over the word *julús*, and the chhátá over *sáhib.*

3. Rupee issued in A.H. 1225 only (A.D. 1810).

INSCRIPTION.

Obverse. سکه مبارک صاحب قران ثانی محمد اکبر شاه بادشاه غازي ١٢٢٥
Sikka mubárak sáhib kirán sány Muhammad Akbar Sháh bádsháh ghází, 1225.

"Auspicious coin of the second *sáhib kirán*, the noble monarch Muhammad Akbar Sháh, A.H. 1225."

Symbols. The chhátá over *sahib.*

Reverse. سنة ۴ جلوس ميمنت مانوس ضرب دهولپور تمنچه راج گوهد
Sanah 4 *julús maimanat mánús zarab Dholpur Tamanchá ráj Gohad.*

"Struck at Dholpur, Tamanchá ráj Gohad, in the 4th year of his fortunate reign."

Symbols. The Tamanchá (pistol) over the word *Dholpur.*

Weight. 172 grains.

4. Tamanchá Sáhí struck in the latter part of Kírat Singh's reign, A.H. 1226–1252 (A.D. 1811–1836). The coins were not issued regularly every year, but as required. See Plate XII. fig. 12.

INSCRIPTION.

Obverse. سکه مبارک صاحب قران ثاني محمد اکبر بادشاه غازي سنة ١٢٥١

Sikka mubárak sáhib kirán sány Muhammad Akbar bádsháh ghází sanah 1251 (A.H.).

"Auspicious coin of the second *sáhib kirán* (lord of the fortunate conjunction of planets), the noble monarch Muhammad Akbar, the year A.H. 1251 (A.D. 1835)."

Symbols. The chhátá over the letters *hb* of *sáhib*.

Reverse. ضرب گوهد سنة ٣٠ جلوس میمنت مانوس

Zarab Gohad sanah 30 *julús maimanat mánús.*

"Struck at Gohad in the 30th year of his fortunate reign."

Symbols. The pistol over the *j* of *julús*, and a triple bow.

Weight. 170 grains.

Value. 16¼ annas Imperial.

5. A coin with the same inscription as No. 4, but with a differently formed chhátá, and the numerals 228 in Persian under the *hb* of *sáhib*, the latter probably a mark of the mint dároga. See Plate XII. fig. 10.

Weight. 170 grains.

In 1857 (A.H. 1274), rupees were issued by Mahárájá Ráná Bhagwant Singh. The old mould (*sáncha*) of Kírat Singh's time was again used. The coins bear the *sanah* 31, A.H. 1252.

No coins have been issued in this State since A.D. 1857.

The chhátá on the coins is the mark of the Dehlí Emperor.

At Dholpur 8 grains of rice make a ratti, 8 rattis make a másha, and 12 máshas go to a tola.